PSYCHOLOGICAL PERSPECTIVES ON THE LIFE OF PAUL

An Application of the Methodology of Gerd Theissen

PSYCHOLOGICAL PERSPECTIVES ON THE LIFE OF PAUL

An Application of the Methodology of Gerd Theissen

Terrance Callan

Studies in the Bible and Early Christianity
Volume 22

The Edwin Mellen Press
Lewiston/Queenston/Lampeter

Library of Congress Cataloging-in-Publication Data

Callan, Terrance, 1947-
   Psychological perspectives on the life of Paul : an application of
the methodology of Gerd Theissen / Terrance D. Callan.
      p.   cm. -- (Studies in the Bible and early Christianity ; v.
22)
   Includes bibliographical references.
   ISBN 0-88946-622-X
   1. Bible. N.T.   Epistles of Paul--Psychology. 2. Paul, the
Apostle, Saint--Psychology.   I. Title. II. Series.
BS2655.P88C34   1990
   225.9'2--dc20   90-33278
                                                                CIP

This is volume 22 in the continuing series
Studies in the Bible and Early Christianity
Volume 22 ISBN 0-88946-622-X
SBEC Series ISBN 0-88946-913-X

A CIP catalog record for this book
is available from the British Library.

All rights reserved. For information contact

The Edwin Mellen Press   The Edwin Mellen Press
         Box 450   Box 67
   Lewiston, New York   Queenston, Ontario
      USA 14092   CANADA L0S 1L0

The Edwin Mellen Press, Ltd.
Lampeter, Dyfed, Wales
UNITED KINGDOM SA48 7DY

Printed in the United States of America

For my parents

CONTENTS

Acknowledgments

I wish to thank several people who have read part, or all, of this manuscript, and made helpful suggestions for its improvement. They deserve some of the credit for its virtues, but naturally none of the blame for its defects. They are Thomas A. Kohut, Thomas L. Kotter, Wayne A. Meeks and James E. Dittes. I also wish to thank the members of the Working Group on Interpretive Approaches to Paul, Eastern Great Lakes Biblical Society, in whose company I worked out many of these ideas.

An earlier form of Chapters 1 and 2 was published as "Competition and Boasting: Toward a Psychological Portrait of Paul" in Studia Theologica 40 (1986) 137-56 and Journal of Religious Studies 13 (1986) 27-51. An earlier form of Chapter 3 appeared as "Toward a Psychological Interpretation of Paul's Sexual Ethic" in Proceedings of the Eastern Great Lakes and Midwestern Biblical Societies, 1986, 57-71.

Biblical quotations are taken from the Revised Standard Version. Whenever possible, quotations from Greek and Latin authors are based on the text and translation of the Loeb Classical Library.

The abbreviations used in what follows are those established by the Journal of Biblical Literature. See "Instructions for Contributors", JBL 107 (1988) 579-96.

Chapter 1

Introduction

A. Previous Psychological Interpretation of Paul

Psychological analysis of the letters of Paul is not something new. Many exegetes, and even some psychologists, have proposed psychological interpretations of Paul, both in passing and at considerable length. The most common focus of such psychological analysis is what is usually called Paul's conversion.[1] In her 1978 dissertation, B. Gaventa surveys the history of discussion of Paul's conversion;[2] many of the explanations of it which she describes involve some psychological analysis.

The most common such analysis is the familiar idea that Paul found himself unable to keep the law of Moses, and in his guilt first persecuted the Christians, who were free of the law, and later accepted such freedom for himself. Often this analysis involves an autobiographical understanding of Romans 7. According to Gaventa, H. J. Holtzmann, A. Deissmann, A. C. McGiffert, W. L. Knox, A. D. Nock, C. H. Dodd, D. M. Davies and P. Carrington are recent advocates of this view.[3] D. W. Riddle and S. Sandmel have also espoused it.[4] And O. Pfister, S. Tarachow and H. Fischer have also interpreted Paul's conversion along these lines, adding that Paul's guilt arose from conflict between Paul's sexual impulses and the law.[5] This analysis of Paul has been convincingly refuted by P. H. Menoud, J. Dupont and K. Stendahl both by exegesis of Romans 7 and by reference to other passages in the letters of Paul, especially Philippians 3.[6]

Gaventa also mentions several other psychological analyses of Paul's conversion. E. G. Selwyn, depending on some remarks of C. G. Jung,[7] argues that Paul persecuted Christians in an attempt to repress an unconscious Christ-complex, and that his conversion was the moment when this complex associated itself with Paul's ego.[8]   J. L. Cheek argues that Paul was experiencing some inner conflict when he had a vision of the death and resurrection of Jesus through which, by means of identification with Jesus, his conscious ego died.[9] Finally, R. Rubenstein argues that Paul was fearful of mortality and was in conflict between his hopes that the messiah had come to defeat mortality and his realistic doubt that this could be so. Rubenstein sees the conversion itself as an ego-failure which Paul eventually integrated by becoming a Christian.[10]

In addition to the interpretation of Paul's conversion mentioned above, C. H. Dodd has also attempted a more general psychological sketch. Dodd describes Paul as being highly strung, having an ardent temperament that took life seriously, with little sense of humor. He had the spiritual constitution that makes the mystic.[11] Dodd also says that Paul needed something to be proud of and was sensitive to humiliation.[12]

Many psychological interpretations of Paul have made use of the ideas of S. Freud and C. G. Jung. G. Theissen has surveyed such interpretations and sees them as focusing on six themes in Paul:[13]

1. Consciousness of sin - S. Freud[14]

2. Conflict over the law - O. Pfister, G. Créspy, A. Vergote[15]
3. Devaluation of the body - H. Fischer, S. Tarachow[16]
4. The doctrine of justification - R. Scroggs, J. J. Forsyth, D. Stollberg[17]
5. Christ mysticism - C. G. Jung, D. Cox, J. G. Bishop, R. Rubenstein, D. Stollberg[18]
6. Paul's social relationships - S. Tarachow, A. Schreiber, E. Fromm[19]

The most recent psychological interpretation of Paul is Theissen's own.[20] Seeking to describe and explain the effects of Pauline theology on human behavior and experience in early Christianity, Theissen analyzes five texts, or groups of texts, from Paul's letters (1 Cor 4:1-5; Rom 2:16; 1 Cor 14:20-25 - 2 Cor 3:4-4:6 - Rom 7:7-23 - 1 Cor 14 - and 1 Cor 2:6-16) and tries to illuminate each from the perspectives of learning theory, depth psychology and cognitive psychology.

Interpretations of Paul's conversion, the essay of Dodd on "The Mind of Paul," and some of the studies listed above in Theissen's categories 2, 3, 5 and 6 are mainly attempts to understand Paul as a person. The rest of the studies listed by Theissen and his own psychological interpretation are mainly attempts to understand Pauline theology. While these two cannot be separated, it is possible to emphasize one or the other. The focus of the present study will be the person of Paul. Since his conversion is psychologically the most significant event of Paul's life known to us, any psychological analysis of Paul must interpret his conversion. But I will attempt also to interpret a broad selection of the data provided by his letters.

B. Methodology

1. Psychohistory - Psychobiography

Recent decades have seen the development of a new, interdisciplinary field of study, a fusion of psychology and history often called psychohistory. The use of psychology in history is not a recent phenomenon,[21] but practitioners of this fusion have become increasingly aware that they are creating a new academic discipline and have reflected much on its methodology.[22] Although all of the psychological interpretation of Paul discussed above falls within the definition of psychohistory, none of it has been undertaken with explicit awareness of this developing field of inquiry. The methodological reflections of psychohistorians, and especially of psychobiographers, should be of assistance in the present attempt to interpret Paul psychologically.

The single most useful discussion of psychobiographical method is J. W. Anderson's essay "The Methodology of Psychological Biography."[23] Like the other methodological studies which Anderson synthesizes, his treatment is mainly negative, arising from criticism of earlier psychobiographical efforts.[24] Anderson lists and discusses six difficulties which beset the psychobiographical enterprise:

1. Reductionism
2. Inflated expectations about what psychobiography can accomplish

3. Disparagement of the subject of the biography
4. Applying contemporary psychology to another era
5. Inadequacies in psychological theory
6. Analyzing an absent subject.

The first two of these difficulties are closely related and can be avoided most of all, as Anderson suggests, by recognition of the complexity of events and of the individual personality,[25] and thus of the limited contribution which psychological analysis can make to their elucidation.[26] In order to avoid the third, it is necessary for the biographer to be aware of his or her own feelings about the subject of the biography and to attempt to develop empathy for that person.[27]

The fourth, fifth and sixth of these difficulties are those which present the greatest problems for a psychological interpretation of Paul. With regard to the fourth, Anderson suggests that an empathic relationship with the subject of one's biography and a thorough knowledge of the subject's culture make it possible to use contemporary psychology to understand someone who lived in another era.[28] T. W. Africa argues this point explicitly with reference to psychohistorical study of the classical period[29] and provides an example of psychobiography of Brutus, one of the assassins of Julius Caesar.[30]

The difficulty posed by inadequacies in psychological theory may be an even greater problem than that of applying contemporary psychological theory to the past. Most psychohistory is psychoanalytic, but psychoanalysis is itself not uniform; its distinct sub-types include H. Kohut's understanding of narcissism and E. Erikson's theories about the life cycle. And psychoanalysis is only one school of psychology. Anderson recommends an eclectic use of psychological theory and modification of it in the light of the biographical subject's unique history.[31]

The difficulty presented by analyzing an absent subject is the greatest obstacle to psychobiography. Without direct access to the subject, the biographer cannot use the ordinary means by which psychologists analyze their clients, e.g., free association. However, Anderson observes that the biographer can make use of information not usually available to the psychologist, e.g., informants other than the subject and the whole pattern of the subject's life. And Anderson points out that the literary materials on which the biography is based can provide psychologically significant data of an unusual kind, e.g., the subject's use of imagery.[32]

2. G. Theissen

Despite his silence concerning psychohistory and his emphasis on a psychological understanding of Pauline theology rather than of Paul as a person, the methodological reflections of G. Theissen provide the most important guidance toward a psychobiography of Paul. Theissen's methodology offers the best hope of overcoming the last three of Anderson's six difficulties besetting psychobiography.

First, Theissen recognizes that the study of psychology itself is pursued in different ways. He identifies and describes three approaches which he calls learning theory, depth psychology and cognitive psychology. Rather than choosing among them, Theissen seeks to combine them and use all three. He proposes that each is concerned with a different level of human experience and behavior. Depth psychology explores the archaic aspects of human experience and behavior; learning theory studies higher forms of individual learning through experience of the surrounding world; and cognitive psychology is concerned with the integration of all experience and behavior into a world of meaning.[33] This is Theissen's solution of the problem of inadequacies in psychological theory.

Second, Theissen considers how it is possible to analyze a text psychologically and identifies three steps in doing so:

1. Description of the psychological aspects of a text with the help of psychological categories

2. Comparison of these psychological aspects with analogies to be found in the cultural milieu of the text in order to avoid projection of modern ideas onto the past

3. Analysis of these psychological aspects of the text by making use of psychological theories.[34]

In this way Theissen attempts to solve the problem of applying contemporary psychology to another era.

Description of the aspects of a text relevant to learning theory and cognitive psychology is fairly straightforward once the appropriate questions are asked. But because depth psychology is based on a distinction between conscious and unconscious mental processes, perception of the depth psychological aspects of a text is more problematic. It depends on locating items in which there is a split between a conscious and an unconscious level of meaning. Theissen identifies six such items:

1. Metaphors used in the text
2. Interpretations of another text which occur in the text
3. Homologies between a mythical presentation of something and the description of the same thing as an inner process
4. The omission of a certain theme where it might be expected and its appearance in a different context
5. Contradictions in the text
6. Over-reactions.[35]

Thus Theissen tries to overcome the difficulty of analyzing an absent subject.

However they may need to be modified in the future, Theissen's reflections on method provide a new starting point for psychological interpretation of Paul, one which is far superior to anything previously available.

*   *   *

In what follows I will use Theissen's methodology, supplemented by the methodological reflections of psychohistorians, to seek understanding of what Paul says on four topics:

1. Competition and boasting
2. Sexuality
3. Parents and children
4. Death.

In each case my principal goal will be to describe Paul's attitude toward the topic. I will be especially concerned to describe the relationship between

conscious and unconscious in Paul. In doing so I will
make use of the six items which Theissen identifies as
revealing an unconscious level of meaning, particularly
contradictions in the text. Then I will compare Paul's
attitude to those of his contemporaries in order to see
Paul, as much as possible, in first century terms.
Finally, I will suggest some ways in which
psychological theories may further illuminate what we
have seen in Paul. Because of the tentative nature of
these psychological interpretations, I will feel
especially free to be eclectic in my use of
psychological theory. However, because it is depth
psychology which has explored the unconscious, I will
appeal most often to psychoanalysis in its various
forms.[36]

My reliance on psychoanalysis has partly
influenced the selection of topics to be discussed. I
begin with competition and boasting because I consider
this the single most prominent element of Paul's letters which seems to have psychological significance.
But I then turn to the topics of sexuality, parents and
children and death not only because of their importance
for Paul, but also because these are psychologically
significant items in psychoanalytic theory. A study of
these topics can hardly be considered a complete
psychological analysis of Paul. But it should shed
considerable light on his personality. And this in
turn may have implications for theological
interpretation of his letters.

Notes

[1]K. Stendahl has recently argued that what happened to Paul was a call rather than a conversion (Paul Among Jews and Gentiles [Philadelphia: Fortress, 1976] 7-23). While I agree that conversion is a misleading and inadequate term, I also think that call is unsatisfactory because it tends to minimize the change Paul experienced. In what follows I will use the familiar term 'conversion' for the sake of convenience.

[2]B. Gaventa, Paul's Conversion: A Critical Sifting of the Epistolary Evidence (Duke University dissertation, 1978) 6-114.

[3]H. J. Holtzmann, Lehrbuch der neutestamentlichen Theologie, 2nd ed., 2 vols. (Freiburg: J. C. B. Mohr, 1897) 2.256; A. Deissmann, Paul: A Study in Social and Religious History, trans. W. E. Wilson, 2nd ed. (London: Hodder and Stoughton, 1926 [German original 1911]) 128-32; A. C. McGiffert, A History of Christianity in the Apostolic Age (New York: Scribner, 1906) 121-5; W. L. Knox, St. Paul and the Church of Jerusalem (Cambridge: University Press, 1925) 46, 117; A. D. Nock, St. Paul (New York: Harper, 1938) 71-2; C. H. Dodd, "The Mind of Paul I," NT Studies (Manchester: University Press, 1953 [original publication 1933]) 74-7; D. M. Davies, "Free from the Law: An Exposition of the Seventh Chapter of Romans," Int 7 (1953) 156; P. Carrington, The Early Christian Church, 2 vols. (Cambridge: University Press, 1957) 1.57-8.

[4]D. W. Riddle, Paul. Man of Conflict: A Modern Biographical Sketch (Nashville: Cokesbury, 1940); S. Sandmel, The Genius of Paul: A Study in History (New York: Schocken, 1970) especially pp 25-35.

[5]O. Pfister, "Die Entwicklung des Apostels Paulus: Eine religionsgeschichtliche und psychologische Skizze," Imago 6 (1920) 243-90, especially pp. 277-9; Christianity and Fear: A Study in History and in the Psychology and Hygiene of Religion trans. by W. H. Johnston (London: Allen and Unwin, 1948) 223-9; S. Tarachow, "St. Paul and Early Christianity: A Psychoanalytic and Historical Study," Psychoanalysis and the Social Sciences 4 (1955) 233; H. Fischer, Gespaltener christlicher Glaube: Eine psychoanalytisch orientierte Religionskritik (Hamburg: Reich, 1974) 56-60.

[6]P. H. Menoud, "Revelation and Tradition: The
Influence of Paul's Conversion on his Theology," Int 7
(1953) 131-41; J. Dupont, "The Conversion of Paul and
its Influence on his Understanding of Salvation by
Faith," Apostolic History and the Gospel, ed. by W. W.
Gasque and R. P. Martin (Grand Rapids, MI: Eerdmans,
1970) 176-94; K. Stendahl, "The Apostle Paul and the
Introspective Conscience of the West," Paul Among Jews
and Gentiles 78-96.   B. J. Malina has developed
Stendahl's argument that Paul does not exhibit an
introspective conscience by proposing that Paul has a
dyadic   self-awareness,   i.e.,   a   self-awareness
emphatically dependent on group embeddedness ("The
Individual and the Community - Personality in the
Social World of Early Christianity," BTB 9 [1979] 126-
38).
    R. H. Gundry ("The Moral Frustration of Paul
Before his Conversion: Sexual Lust in Romans 7:7-25,"
Pauline Studies: Essays Presented to Professor F. F.
Bruce on his 70th Birthday ed. by D. A. Hagner and M.
J. Harris [Grand Rapids, MI: Eerdmans, 1980] 228-45)
argues persuasively that Romans 7 has some autobiographical reference, but in the light of passages
like Philippians 3 Gundry does not think that the moral
frustration reflected in Romans 7 was the decisive
element in Paul's conversion or even an important
element of his personality (pp 233-4).   Similarly,
though on very different grounds, G. Theissen argues
that the 'I' of Romans 7 is typical, but includes Paul
(Psychological Aspects of Pauline Theology, trans. by
J. P. Galvin [Philadelphia: Fortress, 1987] 190-201).
Theissen contends that the experience of the law which
Paul describes in Romans 7 was originally unconscious
and became conscious as a result of Paul's conversion
(pp 222-65).   H. W. Cassirer argues similarly in Grace
and Law: St. Paul, Kant, and the Hebrew Prophets
(Grand Rapids: Eerdmans/Edinburgh: Handsel, 1988) 1-
15.

[7]C. G. Jung, "The Psychological Foundation of
Belief in Spirits," Proceedings of the Society for
Psychical Research 31 (1920), reprinted in The
Collected Works of C. G. Jung, ed. by H. Read, M.
Fordham, G. Adler, 17 vols. (New York: Pantheon, 1960)
8.307-8.

[8]E. G. Selwyn, "St. Stephen's Place in Christian
Origins," Theology 5 (1922) 306-16.   C. G. Inglis also
adopted Jung's interpretation of Paul's conversion,
adding to it that Paul was experiencing conflict over

the law ("The Problem of St. Paul's Conversion," ExpTim 40 [1928-29] 227-31).

[9]J. L. Cheek, "Paul's Mysticism in the Light of Psychedelic Experience," JAAR 38 (1970) 381-9.

[10]R. Rubenstein, My Brother Paul (New York: Harper and Row, 1972) 39-53.

[11]C. H. Dodd, "The Mind of Paul I," 68-70. C. G. Inglis also sees Paul as highly strung and goes on to say that Paul's "tendency towards visions locutions and trances" indicates "that he was psychopathic in temperament" ("The Problem of St. Paul's Conversion," 228).

[12]Dodd, "The Mind of Paul I," 73.

[13]G. Theissen, Psychological Aspects, 25-8.

[14]S. Freud, Moses and Monotheism reprinted in The Standard Edition of the Complete Psychological Works of Sigmund Freud, ed. by J. Strachey (London: Hogarth, 1964) 23.86-7. In studies not mentioned by Theissen, J. A. Sanford (Evil: The Shadow Side of Reality [New York: Crossroad, 1981] 69-76) and W. A. Miller (Make Friends With Your Shadow: How to Accept and Use Positively the Negative Side of Your Personality [Minneapolis: Augsburg, 1981] 72-80) discuss consciousness of sin in Paul in terms of Jungian psychology.

[15]O. Pfister, "Die Entwicklung des Apostel Paulus" [note 5]; G. Créspy, "Exegèse et psychoanalyse. Considerations aventueuses sur Romains 7,7-25," L'evangile, hier et aujourd'hui. Mélanges offerts au Prof. Franz-J. Leenhardt (Geneva: Labor et Fides, 1968) 169-79; A. Vergote, "Der Beitrag der Psychoanalyse zur Exegese. Leben, Gesetz und Ich-Spaltung im 7. Kapitel des Römerbriefs," Exegese im Methodenkonflikt. Zwischen Geschichte und Struktur, ed. by X. Leon-Dufour (Munich: Kösel, 1973) 73-116.

[16]H. Fischer, Gespaltener christlicher Glaube [note 5]; S. Tarachow, "St. Paul and Early Christianity" [note 5].

[17]R. Scroggs, "The Heuristic Value of the Psychoanalytic Model in the Interpretation of Paul," Zygon 13 (1978) 136-57; J. J. Forsyth, "Faith and Eros:

Paul's Answer to Freud," Religion in Life 46 (1977) 476-87; D. Stollberg, "Tiefenpsychologie oder historisch-kritische Exegese? Identität und der Tod des Ich (Gal 2:19-20)," Doppeldeutlich. Tiefendimensionen biblischer Texte, ed. by Y. Spiegel (Munich: Kaiser, 1978) 215-26.

[18]C. G. Jung, "The Psychological Foundation of Belief in Spirits" [note 7]; D. Cox, Jung and St. Paul: A Study of the Doctrine of Justification by Faith and its Relation to the Concept of Individuation (London: Longmans, Green, 1959); J. G. Bishop, "Psychological Insights in St. Paul's Mysticism," Theology 78 (1975) 318-24; R. Rubenstein, My Brother Paul [note 10]; D. Stollberg, "Tiefenpsychologie oder historisch-kritische Exegese?"

[19]S. Tarachow, "St. Paul and Early Christianity;" A. Schreiber, Die Gemeinde in Korinth. Versuch einer gruppendynamische Betrachtung der Entwicklung der Gemeinde von Korinth auf der Basis des ersten Korintherbriefes (Munster: Aschendorf, 1977): E. Fromm, "Die Entstehung des Christusdogmas. Eine psychoanalytische Studie zur socialpsychologischen Funktion der Religion," Imago 16 (1930) 305-73.

[20]G. Theissen, Psychological Aspects.

[21]On this see F. E. Manuel, "The Use and Abuse of Psychology in History," Daedalus 100 (1971) 187-212.

[22]See W. J. Gilmore, Psychohistorical Inquiry: A Comprehensive Research Bibliography (Garland Reference Library of Social Science, 156; New York and London: Garland, 1984), especially pp 6-86. Helpful reviews of psychohistorical works include H. Kohut, "Beyond the Bounds of the Basic Rule," Journal of the American Psychoanalytic Association 8 (1960) 567-86; and J. E. Mack, "Psychoanalysis and Historical Biography," Ibid. 19 (1971) 143-79.

[23]Journal of Interdisciplinary History 11 (1981) 455-75.

[24]For a more positive statement of psycho-biographical method see E. Erikson, "On the Nature of Psycho-Historical Evidence: In Search of Gandhi," Daedalus 97 (1968) 695-730. Some of what Erikson says is not applicable to the study of a figure from the distant past.

[25]J. W. Anderson, "Methodology," 457-60.

[26]Ibid. 460-61.

[27]Ibid. 464-5.

[28]Ibid. 466-7. On this see also P. Gay, Freud for Historians (New York/Oxford: Oxford University Press, 1985) 78-115.

[29]"Psychohistory, Ancient History, and Freud: The Descent into Avernus," Arethusa 12 (1979) 5-33. See E. R. Dodds, The Greeks and the Irrational (Sather Classical Lectures, 25; Berkeley: University of California Press, 1959) for a notably successful use of psychology to understand the classical period. R. Scroggs has argued for use of psychology to interpret the Bible, though he excludes biographical applications ("Psychology as a Tool to Interpret the Text," The Christian Century, March 24, 1982, 335-8).

[30]"The Mask of an Assassin: A Psychohistorical Study of M. Junius Brutus," Journal of Interdisciplinary History 8 (1978) 599-626. Other psychobiographies of figures contemporary with Paul include G. Maranon, Tiberius the Resentful Caesar trans. by W. B. Wells (New York: Duell, Sloan and Pearce, 1956); M. Rozelaar, "Seneca: A New Approach to his Personality," Psychiatry 36 (1973) 82-92; and most recently J. W. Miller, "Jesus' 'Age Thirty Transition': A Psychohistorical Probe," SBLSP 1985, 45-56. From a later period Augustine has been the subject of numerous psychobiographical essays. Notable among them are E. R. Dodds, "Augustine's Confessions: A Study in Spiritual Maladjustment," Hibbert Journal 26 (1927) 459-73; P. Fredriksen, "Augustine and his Analysts: The Possibility of a Psychohistory," Soundings 61 (1978) 206-27; and most recently P. Rigby, "Paul Ricoeur, Freudianism, and Augustine's Confessions," JAAR 53 (1985) 93-114; and D. Capps, "Augustine as Narcissist: Comments on Paul Rigby's 'Paul Ricoeur, Freudianism, and Augustine's Confessions,'" Ibid. 115-27.

[31]J. W. Anderson, "Methodology," 467-70.

[32]Ibid. 470-74. See also P. Gay, Freud for Historians, 181-212. For an example of psychological analysis based on letters see A. Baldwin, "Personal Structure Analysis: A Statistical Method for In-

vestigating the Single Personality," _Journal_ _of_ _Abnormal_ _and_ _Social_ _Psychology_ 37 (1942) 163-83.

[33]G. Theissen, _Psychological_ _Aspects_, 51.

[34]_Ibid_. 45-6, 49. See also the outline of _Psychological_ _Aspects_, Parts 2-6.

[35]_Ibid_. 46-8.

[36]P. Gay attempts to argue that psychoanalysis is the best psychological approach for the historian to use (_Freud_ _for_ _Historians_, 42-77).

Chapter 2

Competition and Boasting

A. Paul the Competitor

1. Pre-Christian Period

In Paul's brief references to his life before
becoming a follower of Jesus, he gives us reason to
believe that comparison of himself with others and
competition with them was an important element of his
personality at that time.[1] In Gal 1:14 he explicitly
compares his pre-Christian self with his contemporaries
and says that he surpassed them - "I advanced in
Judaism beyond many of my own age among my people, so
extremely zealous was I for the traditions of my
fathers." The same thing emerges almost as clearly in
Phil 3:4-6 where Paul argues that he has greater reason
for confidence in the flesh than others do (v 4).
After mentioning his circumcision on the 8th day, he
enumerates in v 5 some foundations for confidence in
the flesh which are his by virtue of birth, i.e., being
of the people of Israel, of the tribe of Benjamin, a
Hebrew of the Hebrews.[2] Then in v 5-6 he lists three
reasons for confidence in the flesh which are his own
achievement: "as to the law a Pharisee," i.e., a
member of an observant group of Jews; "as to zeal a
persecutor of the church," i.e., so ardent that he took
the extreme step of persecuting; and "as to
righteousness under the law blameless," i.e., a perfect
Jew.[3]

Not only do these passages tell us that Paul compared himself with others and competed with them; they also tell us that Paul's competition took the form of outdoing others in zeal (zelos) for Judaism (cf. also Acts 22:3). This word and its cognates have been studied by A. Stumpff.[4] According to Stumpff the basic meaning of zelos is "the capacity or state of passionate committal to a person or cause," which can be a good or a bad quality. When it is a good quality, this passionate commitment is 'zeal' or 'enthusiasm;' as a bad quality it is 'contention' or 'jealousy.'[5] But when zelos was used to translate qn'h and its cognates in the Greek translation of the Hebrew scriptures, it took on new meaning. Most strikingly, it was frequently imputed to God in the sense of 'jealousy,' indicating God's exclusive claim on, and commitment to, Israel.[6] And then, in dependence on this usage, zelos was occasionally imputed to men with the implication that they are "representatively...filled by this holy zeal for the maintaining of the divine glory..."[7]

According to Stumpff, Paul uses zelos in this last sense in the passages we are considering.[8] If so, then it may be that Paul's striving to excel, taking the form of surpassing zeal, was authorized and strengthened by being identified with the zeal of God himself. This would help to explain the otherwise surprising fact that Paul was a persecutor. Identification with the zeal of God might lead to actions which would be unlikely as actions of a mere human being. Such identification is explicit in the case of Phineas, the prototype of religious zeal. After Phineas has killed Zimri and the Midianite woman

as they lay together, God says that Phineas was zealous
with the zeal of God (Num 25:11).

2. Christian Period

It seems clear that one result of Paul's
conversion was that he became critical of his own
propensity to compare himself with others and compete
with them. It is probable that this is so because such
competition is an expression of self-reliance, and in
his conversion Paul was profoundly convinced that
righteousness was a free gift and could not be earned.
Consequently he eschewed self-reliance and with it
competition. This is fairly explicit in Phil 3:3-11.
After enumerating his reasons for confidence in the
flesh in v 4-6 (as we have seen), Paul goes on in v 7
to say that whatever gain he had, he counted as loss
for the sake of Christ. And then in v 9 he says that
he has given up trying to establish his own
righteousness by keeping the law, and now looks for
righteousness which comes through faith (in Christ).
Thus Paul simultaneously turns his back on self-
reliance and on competition with others in the effort
to establish his own righteousness.[9]

However, it is also clear that even as a Christian
Paul did continue to rely on himself and compete with
others despite his arguments against doing so. A
particularly illuminating example of this inconsistency
is found in 1 Cor 15:10.[10] Paul says

> By the grace of God I am what I am [i.e., an
> apostle], and his grace toward me was not in
> vain. On the contrary, I worked harder than
> any of them [i.e., the other apostles],

though it was not I, but the grace of God
which is with me.

After first claiming that he worked harder than
any of the other apostles, Paul corrects himself and
says that it was not his doing, but the grace of God.
From this we can see that Paul did not want to rely on
himself and compete with others after his conversion.
But the passage shows just as clearly that despite this
desire Paul did continue to rely on himself and compete
as a Christian, since he does claim to have worked
harder than the other apostles. And it suggests that
Paul is partly unconscious of this continuing self-
reliance and competition because the statement is also
a mis-statement, a slip of tongue or pen, which Paul
corrects.[11]   Finally, this passage also shows that
insofar as he was aware that he continued to rely on
himself and compete with others, Paul could allow for
this by attributing it not to himself, but to the grace
of God, i.e., by identifying his striving with the
action of God's grace in him. Thus both before and
after he became a Christian, Paul identified his
efforts with the action of God in him; however, this
was not in the former case, as it was in the latter, a
way of allowing for such effort despite a critical
attitude toward it.

If we look only at Paul's final statement, 1 Cor
15:10 is simply one expression of his well-known view
that human effort, his own and others', does have a
place in Christian life as a response to the free gift
of righteousness.[12]   This stands in a dialectical
tension with Paul's critique of self-reliance, but is
not inconsistent with it. But 1 Cor 15:10 also shows
that Paul's pre-Christian attitude of self-reliance,

expressed in competition, persisted in him unconsciously and that it was inconsistent with his critique of self-reliance. Insofar as Paul becomes conscious of it (as he does in 1 Cor 15:10), he can allow for it by identifying it with the action of God in him. But insofar as it remains unconscious, it makes Paul inconsistent with himself.

The picture of Paul which emerges from 1 Cor 15:10 is confirmed by a variety of themes running through his letters. These show that despite his critique of self-reliance and competition, as a Christian Paul continued to rely on himself and compete unconsciously, and that insofar as he was conscious of it he authorized it by identifying with God and/or Christ.[13]

a) use of athletic imagery

In a number of places Paul applies the image of athletic competition to himself[14] and others (1 Cor 9:24-7; Gal 5:7). V. C. Pfitzner argues that Paul's point in using this image is not to approve or promote competition.[15] However, even if it is not his conscious intent, the use of such imagery, which is intimately connected with rivalry and self-assertion,[16] seems to show that Paul unconsciously saw himself and other Christians as self-reliant and competitive.

b) fear of failure

In connection with several of these uses of an athletic image Paul expresses concern that he may have run in vain (Gal 2:2; Phil 2:16) or be found wanting (adokimos - 1 Cor 9:27). Similarly, Paul is elsewhere concerned that he may have labored in vain (Gal 4:11; Phil 2:16; 1 Thess 3:5), boasted in vain (2 Cor 9:3-4) or be found wanting (adokimos - 2 Cor 13:6). This concern may be expressed obliquely when Paul denies that the grace of God toward him has been in vain (1 Cor 15:10; cf. 15:58) or that his work has been in vain (1 Thess 2:1). As is unambiguous in the context of athletic imagery and in 1 Cor 15:10, it seems that these expressions of fear of failure are a negative reflection of Paul's unconsciously continuing to rely on himself and compete as a Christian.[17]

c) mimesis of Paul

Paul frequently presents himself as a model to be imitated. In 1 Thess 1:6 he says that the Thessalonians have become imitators of him, and in 1 Cor 4:16 he urges the Corinthians to imitate him.[18] He says to the Galatians "become as I am" (4:12), to the Corinthians "I wish that all were as I myself am" (1 Cor 7:7) and to the Philippians "what you have...heard and seen in me, do" (4:9).

Paul's presentation of himself as a model seems to proceed from, and reflect, his sense of himself as a person of notable achievement. It also seems to presuppose that this achievement will, or should, be recognized by others.[19] Paul was at least partly conscious of this, and insofar as he was, he validated it by means of identification with Christ. Thus in 1 Thess 1:6 he says "you became imitators of us and of the Lord," and in 1 Cor 11:1 he says "be imitators of me, as I am of Christ."

d) disdain

A negative counterpart to Paul's presentation of himself as a model is his occasional expression of disdain for his peers. The clearest example is in Gal 2:1-10 where he repeatedly calls the leaders of the Jerusalem church hoi dokountes (v 2, 6, 9). This term is used both positively and negatively or ironically.[20] That Paul uses it ironically here is clear from v 6 where he says that what the dokountes were does not matter to him because God shows no partiality. Paul does not deny the position of the dokountes, but at the same time does not consider it to be important. Therefore it seems very likely that he uses the term dokountes to indicate a disparity between appearance and reality: the leaders of the Jerusalem church appear to be something, and are insofar as they are recognized as such, but in reality their worth depends not on what they appear to be, but on what they are in the judgment of God.[21] Paul's emphatic disdain for the apparent importance of these leaders seems to reflect Paul's sense that he is at least their equal and can assess their worth. Paul here again reveals that he compares himself with others and competes with them, and further, that at times he thinks little of them.

The same thing is reflected even more strikingly in the following story of Paul's confrontation with Cephas in Antioch (Gal 2:11-14). Paul's public calling of Cephas to account for hypocrisy rather clearly implies that Paul is his equal and that at least in this instance Paul has no great respect for him.

Closely parallel to Paul's use of dokountes in Galatians 2 is his description of apostles as hyperlian in 2 Cor 11:5 and 12:11. The term is ironic[22] and expresses doubt about the self-evaluation of Paul's opponents and their evaluation by the Corinthians, by exaggerating it. Paul's disdain for these opponents again seems to reflect Paul's view of himself as their equal or better. Again we see that Paul sometimes thinks little of those with whom he competes.

Paul is at least partly conscious of the competitive character of this disdain and justifies it by identifying with God. In Gal 2:6 he bases his disdain for the dokountes on the impartiality of God, clearly implying that God's attitude is also his.

e) zelos

As might be expected, because zeal was so large a part of what Paul after his conversion regarded as reprehensible striving for superiority, as a Christian Paul is critical of zeal, though not as critical as he is of the striving for superiority itself. This is clear from Rom 10:2 where Paul testifies that non-Christian Israel has zeal for God (or the zeal of God), but it is not enlightened (cf. Gal 4:17-18). In v 3 he explains that this is so because they attempt to establish their own righteousness. It seems very likely that Paul would apply this same critique to his own pre-conversion zeal. But this critique seems to imply the possibility of an enlightened zeal, one which is not part of an attempt to establish one's own righteousness (cf. 1 Cor 12:31; 14:1, 39).

That Paul as a Christian was characterized by such zeal is clear from 2 Cor 11:2 where Paul tells the Corinthians that he is zealous for them with the zeal of God. Here Paul compares his competition with his rivals in Corinth for the loyalty of the Corinthians to God's competition with idols for the loyalty of Israel. In this case Paul is consciously competitive, his

competition takes the form of zeal, and this zeal is
validated by being understood as a participation in the
zeal of God.

*   *   *

From all of this it seems clear that after Paul
became a Christian, despite a critical attitude toward
self-reliance and competition with others, Paul
continued to strive to excel.   In part he was
unconscious of this and so, unknowingly, inconsistent.
Unconsciously Paul remained the very sort of person he
preached against, which is perhaps not at all
surprising psychologically.[23] Insofar as he was aware
of his continuing self-reliance and competition, Paul
could accept it by identifying with God and Christ, and
his striving with their action in and through him.
This stood in dialectical tension with his critique of
self-reliance and competition, but was not inconsistent
with it and allowed the expression of the competitive
element of his personality.

B.   Paul's Boasting

All the elements of the picture outlined thus far
are confirmed and elaborated when we examine the theme
of boasting in Paul.[24] Boasting is intimately related
to the self-reliant, competitive character which we
have discovered in Paul; one who is motivated by a
desire to surpass one's peers might very readily boast
of success in doing so.   As we might expect on the
basis of the foregoing, Paul is critical of any
boasting about oneself, yet continues to boast.[25] In
part this is unconscious; but insofar as it is

conscious, Paul justifies it by identifying with Jesus - he boasts of his accomplishments as a servant of the Lord.

Paul's clearest statement of opposition to boasting is found in Rom 3:27 - "Then what becomes of our boasting? It is excluded."[26] (Cf. Rom 4:2; Eph 2:9). Yet Paul continues to boast. Some of this is not boasting about himself, but about God and/or Christ, as is recommended in Jer 9:23 (LXX 9:24), paraphrased in 1 Cor 1:31 - "Let the one who boasts, boast in the Lord." This boasting in the Lord is the exact opposite of the boasting about righteousness achieved through fidelity to the law which is excluded by Rom 3:27 and 4:2. Thus in Gal 6:13-14 Paul accuses his opponents of wanting the Galatians to be circumcised so that they may boast of the Galatians' flesh, while Paul himself boasts only in the cross of Christ. In Phil 3:3 Paul argues against circumcision by saying that Christians boast in Jesus Christ and put no confidence in the flesh. And in 1 Cor 1:26-31 Paul argues against boasting of any quality or accomplishment which might be considered the basis for God's call; rather, one should boast in the Lord. (Cf. also Rom 5:2, 11).

However, not all of Paul's boasting is such boasting in the Lord. He can also boast of his accomplishments. This may be partly unconscious, as when he refers to the Thessalonians as his crown of boasting before the Lord Jesus at his coming (1 Thess 2:19) and exhorts the Philippians to faithfulness so that he can boast of not laboring in vain on the day of Christ (Phil 2:16). But it is also clearly conscious

at times, and then Paul is able to justify it by giving
another meaning to boasting in the Lord. When Paul
paraphrases Jer 9:23 in 2 Cor 10:17, the boasting which
is excluded is boasting in the work of others (2 Cor
10:15); boasting in the Lord, on the other hand, seems
to mean boasting of one's accomplishment of the
missionary work assigned by the Lord (10:13; cf. v 16).
Similarly in Rom 15:17-18 Paul speaks of boasting in
Christ Jesus about what Christ has done through him.
Thus boasting in the Lord can include not only boasting
in the free gift of righteousness through Christ, but
also boasting in one's own accomplishments in the
service of Christ.

R. Bultmann argues that there is no contradiction
between Paul's basic rejection of boasting and the idea
that one may boast of one's achievements as a servant
of Christ, since the latter does not involve comparison
of oneself with others.[27] In Gal 6:4 Paul does
advocate having one's reason to boast in oneself rather
than in another, and in 2 Cor 10:12 he says that he
does not compare himself with his opponents. But as we
have already seen, despite such statements it is clear
that Paul did continue to compare himself with others
as a Christian, and that he reconciled this with his
critique of boasting by identifying his own strivings
with the grace of God.[28]

Boasting in Corinth

This complex combination of criticism of boasting
and continuing to boast, both consciously and
unconsciously, with the conscious boasting warranted by
identification with God and Christ, appears with

special clarity in the Corinthian correspondence. Boasting seems to have been a focal issue in Paul's relations with the Corinthians; 34 of Paul's 50 explicit references to boasting are found in these two letters.

It is clear that one of Paul's concerns in 1 Corinthians is to counter the Corinthians' tendency to boast. They are boasting both about their connection with various apostles (3:21-2; cf. 1:12; 3:4) and about themselves (4:7; 5:6; cf. 3:18). The former has created factions in the Corinthian community (1:10-11) which is the problem Paul is trying to resolve in 1 Corinthians 1-4. But it is clear that in his opinion boasting about apostles is intimately related to the Corinthians' boasting about themselves (cf. especially 3:18-23). Paul categorically excludes the latter in 1:29 where he concludes the description of the Corinthians as not being very notable by the standards of the world (v 26-8) by saying that God has chosen such people "so that no human being might boast in the presence of God." And he supports this in v 31 by paraphrasing Jer 9:23 (LXX 9:24) as we have noted above. He also argues that they should not boast about themselves in 4:7 and 5:6 (cf. 3:18).[29] Paul argues explicitly that the Corinthians should not boast about apostles in 3:21-2. This is the conclusion of an argument in 3:5-17 that Paul and Apollos are merely servants of God and therefore not to be boasted about. Paul returns to this point in 4:1-5.

In view of this complete rejection of boasting, it is particularly striking that Paul also boasts in 1 Corinthians. It is boasting in the Lord no doubt, but not in the narrow sense suggested by 1 Cor 1:31, i.e., boasting in what God has done in Christ. Instead Paul boasts of what he has done as a servant of Christ. A somewhat oblique instance of this is Paul's argument in 1:17-3:4 that he consciously chose not to preach the gospel with eloquent wisdom among the Corinthians (1:17; 2:1-5), but that there is a wisdom of God which he could have imparted to them (2:6-7) if they had been ready for it (3:1-4). More explicitly, in 15:31 Paul refers to the Corinthians as the boast which he has in Christ Jesus. In 15:10 as we have already seen, he 'boasts' of his work as an apostle and then immediately corrects himself and attributes it to the grace of God. And in 9:15-18 he refers to his preaching of the gospel free of charge as a ground for boasting. This may well be an instance of unconscious boasting since there is no explicit reference to identification with God or Christ.[30] In any case Paul seems unconscious of the contradiction between his argument that boasting is absolutely excluded for the Corinthians, and his own continuing to boast.

This suggests an admittedly speculative explanation for the Corinthians' tendency to boast. It may be that when he was with them, Paul displayed the same inconsistency which we can see in 1 Corinthians: on the one hand telling them that boasting was excluded, and on the other hand boasting both consciously of his accomplishments as a servant of the Lord, and unconsciously. If so, his example may have had greater influence than his doctrine, leading the Corinthians to boast themselves and opening the possibility that they would compare Paul with other apostles, not necessarily to his credit.[31] Thus Paul himself may have made an important contribution to the problem of the boasting of the Corinthians, to which he tries to respond in 1 Corinthians.[32]

Whatever may have been the origin of the problem of the Corinthians' boasting, it is clear that 1 Corinthians did not fully resolve it, at least partly because of the arrival in Corinth of apostles whose boasts, accepted by the Corinthians, seemed to make them superior to Paul.   It is also clear that Paul tried a different approach in 2 Corinthians.   The frontal attack on boasting of 1 Corinthians has been replaced in 2 Corinthians by appeals for the Corinthians to boast in Paul (1:14; 5:12; cf. 12:11). He bolsters this by boasting in the Corinthians,[33] which as S. Olson has suggested, may be a rhetorical device designed to persuade the readers to agree to Paul's request,[34] most basically that they boast in him, but also that they maintain good relations generally (7:4, 14) and especially that they contribute to the collection (8:24; 9:2-3). However, the main way in which Paul tries to persuade the Corinthians to boast in him is by developing a new understanding of the boasting proper for a Christian, i.e., boasting in weakness; this is implicit in 2:14-7:4 and explicit in 10-13.   This may have been necessary because Paul's rivals could point to greater accomplishments as servants of the Lord than Paul himself could, forcing him to re-define Christian boasting in a way that allows him to make his the stronger case.   As always Paul authorizes this new type of boasting by identifying himself with Christ, in this case with the weakness and suffering of Christ (cf. 4:7-11).   But even as Paul tries to shift the grounds of argument, perhaps because of the urgency of the situation he continues to boast both unconsciously, and consciously as a servant of the Lord,[35] and seems mostly unaware of the inconsistency between these boasts of achievement and his new view that one should boast of weakness.

Paul's inconsistent continuing to boast of achievement even as he calls for boasting in weakness manifests itself in various ways. At times he simply asserts his equality to his rivals on their own terms. At other times he criticizes his rivals' boasts as he presents his own. In both of these cases Paul seems at some times to boast unconsciously and at other times to boast consciously of his achievements as a servant of the Lord, though without realizing that this is inconsistent with the idea that the proper boast is boasting in weakness. And when Paul makes his argument for boasting in weakness, he mentions his achievements before going on to say that he will not boast in them, but only in weakness. At this point he is conscious of what he is doing and feels that this boasting of accomplishment (and implicitly that of his opponents) is inappropriate and inconsistent, as his description of it as foolishness shows.[36]

a) Paul's assertion of equality to his rivals

An example of Paul's assertion of equality to his rivals can be found in 2 Cor 5:12. Here Paul denies that he is commending himself and at the same time tries to give the Corinthians grounds for boasting about him so that they will have something to say to those who boast in appearance. It is clear that Paul is responding to unfavorable comparison of himself with others and that he is trying to give the Corinthians reason to think he is at least the equal of his rivals. The reason which he offers them is apparently his persuasion of men (5:11) which requires that he be in his right mind (v 13). The contradiction between his claim not to be commending himself and this offer of a reason for boasting, suggests that Paul is not fully conscious of what he is doing here.[37]   Cf. also 6:3-10.

Similarly but more consciously, in 10:1-11 Paul responds to the criticism that he is humble (v 1) and weak (v 10) when he is with them (a criticism presumably based on unfavorable comparison of Paul with his rivals) by asserting that he can be bold when he is with them (v 2) and just as strong as he is in his letters (v 10-11). This assertion he refers to as boasting in the authority which the Lord gave him (v 8; cf. 13:10). And in 3:1-3, apparently responding to unfavorable comparison with his rivals on the grounds that he lacks the letters of recommendation which they possess, Paul asserts his equality by claiming that the Corinthians themselves are his letter of recommendation from Christ. A more explicit assertion of equality to his rivals is found in 11:5 where Paul says that he is not at all inferior to the superlative apostles.[38]   In the following verse he goes on to admit an inferiority in speech, but not in knowledge, which he apparently assumes, is what really matters. Similarly in 12:11 he asserts his equality to the superlative apostles and spells that out in the following verse as meaning that he performed all the signs of an apostle for the Corinthians.

b) Paul's criticism of his opponents' boast as he
presents his own

The second way in which Paul continues to boast of
his achievements, i.e., criticizing his opponents'
boast while he presents his own, can be found in 10:12-
18. Here Paul criticizes his rivals for commending
themselves (v 12, 18) and thus failing to act in accord
with Jer 9:23 (LXX 9:24) (v 17). More specifically he
criticizes them of measuring themselves by themselves
and so boasting without limit (v 12-13).[39] Yet more
specifically he criticizes them for boasting in
another's labor (v 15); i.e., they have boasted in what
they have done in Corinth even though Paul, not they,
first brought the gospel to Corinth. Paul on the other
hand, does not commend himself, but is commended by the
Lord (v 18), and his boast is a boast in the Lord in
accordance with Jer 9:23 (v 17). His boast is not
without limit (v 13, 15), but is in accord with the
measure established by God (v 13); i.e., he boasts in
bringing the gospel to Corinth where it had not been
before.[40]

A second instance of combining criticism of the
boast of Paul's rivals with a statement of his own
boast is found in 11:7-15. Here Paul refutes the claim
of his rivals to have the same boast as he does (v 12)
by boasting of not accepting support from the
Corinthians (v 9-10), a boast which he also must defend
to them (v 7, 10; cf. 12:13-15).

c) Paul's argument for boasting in weakness

Paul's explicit argument for boasting in weakness
is found in 11:16-12:10. Here Paul begs the indulgence
of the Corinthians to allow him to boast. This will be

a foolish boast of worldly things (11:17-18). Twice he
begins to boast of his credentials, arguing that he is
equal, or superior, to his rivals. In 11:22-3 he
boasts of being a Hebrew, an Israelite, a descendant of
Abraham, a servant of God;[41] and in 12:1 he boasts of
visions and revelations.[42] But in both cases as he
develops his theme, he ends by boasting of weakness
(11:30; 12:5, 9-10). It is clear that Paul here
develops a new understanding of boasting in the Lord.
There is an anticipation of this in Paul's statements
about boasting in the cross of Christ (Gal 6:14) and
about boasting in God's choice of the Corinthians even
though they are not especially creditable in the eyes
of the world (1 Cor 1:28-31). But in 2 Corinthians
Paul takes a step further and boasts not only in God
who acts through the surprising weakness of the cross
and chooses the weak, but also in his own weakness in
which God is present and active. This turns upside
down the ordinary idea of boasting, including Paul's
own earlier understanding of boasting in the Lord. Now
boasting is not a presentation of success, not even
success as a servant of God, but of failure in which
God's success is somehow to be found. Paul gives one
indication of how he understands this in 2 Cor 4:7-11
where he says that the value of human weakness is that
it makes it clear that God is the source of any power
(cf. 12:9-10).[43] He has a slightly different idea in
Rom 5:3 where he says that we boast of our sufferings
because they produce endurance, etc.

We can imagine that Paul's new understanding of
boasting stems from viewing boasting in the light of
his belief that the Christian is one with Christ, and
that all of Christian life is assimilated to the

pattern of the death and resurrection of Christ (this is explicit in 2 Cor 4:7-11). Theologically this is very significant. But psychologically it is more significant that as Paul presents this new boasting in weakness, he also presents his straightforward boasts. As is the case in 1 Cor 15:10 where Paul first mentions his achievement and then credits it to the Lord, Paul here mentions his achievements and then boasts of his weakness.

*   *   *

1 and 2 Corinthians thus abundantly illustrate Paul's opposition to boasting and yet continuing to do it, both unconsciously and consciously under the aegis of identification with God and Christ. In 1 Corinthians we see that Paul boasts, in part unconsciously, even as he tries to persuade the Corinthians not to boast. In 2 Corinthians, because his argument in 1 Corinthians was not successful, Paul tries to regain the loyalty of the Corinthians by arguing that the proper Christian boasting is boasting in weakness. But perhaps because of the urgency of the situation, Paul also boasts straightforwardly even more than he had in 1 Corinthians, and Paul is apparently only partly aware of this inconsistency. Thus Paul's new understanding of boasting does not result from a resolution of Paul's conflict over this issue, but rather shows the conflict being worked out in a new way.[44]

*   *   *

Our examination of competition and boasting in Paul suggests that Paul was by nature a person who relied on himself, compared himself with others and

competed with them. This led him to seek to excel in
zeal, understood as a participation in God's own zeal,
and this in turn led to his persecution of the
followers of Jesus.

When Paul himself became a follower of Jesus, he
also became critical of this competitive, self-reliant
attitude in himself (and others), both because it had
led him astray, making him a persecutor, and because in
his conversion Paul became convinced that salvation was
entirely a gift. Presumably he tried to change this
attitude, but in this he was only partly successful.
He continued to rely on himself and compete with others
unconsciously. He also did so consciously, justifying
this by identifying his striving with the action of God
in him.

This conflict between the demands of faith and
Paul's basic personality also comes to light in
connection with boasting. Paul says that boasting is
excluded, but continues to boast, both unconsciously,
and consciously on the basis that boasting of one's
accomplishments as a servant of the Lord is boasting in
the Lord, which is permitted for a Christian. In the
conflict of which we have evidence in 2 Corinthians,
perhaps because he encounters others who boast of their
accomplishments in the service of God, Paul develops a
new understanding of boasting in the Lord as meaning
boasting in weakness. But Paul's basic personality
still asserts itself as he continues boasting of his
strength.

Thus the picture of Paul that emerges here is that
of man in conflict - a conflict between his faith and
his basic personality. This conflict may explain part

of the difficulty of understanding Paul both in ancient times and now.   One way to sum up this conflict is to say that Paul himself was the sort of person, at least in his basic tendencies, that he most vigorously criticized, i.e., a self-reliant and self-promoting person.

Having described this conflict at some length, I will discuss briefly the relationship between Paul's attitude toward competition and boasting and the attitudes toward them which can be found in his cultural context.   Then I will suggest a psychological interpretation of Paul's attitude.

C.   Competition and Boasting in Paul's Cultural Milieu

To the 20th century Western reader it may seem that Paul's competitive, boastful character is the main item in our portrait of him which is in need of psychological explanation.   However, it seems likely that such a character was typical of Paul's culture and thus that no special explanation of it is required, unless such an explanation would apply to the entire culture.   B. J. Malina argues that first century Mediterranean culture was an agonistic culture, characterized by competition for honor.[45]   In support of this we may observe that Paul's use of athletic imagery and his presentation of himself as a model to be imitated, two of the things which, I argued, reveal his competitive character, have abundant parallels in his day.[46]   With regard to boasting, H. D. Betz argues that Paul's boasting does not violate the rules governing proper boasting which are found in Plutarch's treatise On Inoffensive Self-Praise.[47]

If it is true that the basic character which we have perceived in Paul is typical of his culture, then what most needs explanation is his critique of self-reliance, competition and boasting. Of course, some critique of at least the last of these is reflected in Plutarch's recognition that self-praise can be offensive. However, for him it is offensive when it detracts from, rather than enhances, one's honor; this is very different from Paul's critique.[48]

A much closer parallel to Paul's critique of boasting is provided by Jewish literature.[49] Although Wisdom literature speaks of boasting about one's accomplishments with approval (e.g., Prov 16:31; Sir 30:2), the Deuteronomic history, psalms and prophetic writings are critical of such boasting (e.g., Judg 7:2; Ps 49:7-8). Especially important is Jer 9:22-3 (LXX 9:23-24) which Paul twice paraphrases:

> Let not the wise man glory in his wisdom, let not the mighty man glory in his might, let not the rich man glory in his riches; but let him who glories glory in this, that he understands and knows me....

We also find criticism of boasting about one's accomplishments in the Testaments of the Twelve Patriarchs (e.g., T. Judah 13.2) and especially in Philo, although Philo makes little use of kauchasthai and its cognates. However, in Spec. Leg. 1.311 Philo says, referring to Deut 10:21, "Let God alone be your boast (auchema)...and be magnified neither in wealth, nor in glory, nor dominion, nor comeliness of body, nor strength...."

If Paul was aware of this attitude toward boasting in the Bible and among his contemporaries before his conversion, he at least did not regard it as incompatible with his attempt to surpass others in zeal for the law nor, quite possibly, with boasting of his success in doing so. However, as a result of his conversion Paul explicitly embraced this critical attitude toward boasting, at least as expressed in Jer 9:22-3, and did understand it as excluding boasting about fulfillment of the law, as well as about any other human accomplishment. Since Paul's conversion was the source of his critique of self-reliance, competition and boasting, a psychological explanation of this critique must be, in effect, a psychological interpretation of his conversion.

D.   Psychological Analysis of Paul's Attitude Toward Competition and Boasting

One psychological framework which seems helpful for understanding Paul's conversion is E. H. Erikson's theory that youth is the time during which a person's ego identity is formed and that this occurs by means of experimentation with various identities.[50] Thus Paul's earlier identity was that of one zealous for the traditions of his fathers, an identity supported by his unconscious identification with the zeal of God. This identity allowed unhindered expression of Paul's competitive, boastful character; and with the intolerance typical of the period of identity formation,[51] Paul persecuted the Christians.

In his conversion Paul exchanged this earlier identity for another. Paul's encounter with the risen

Jesus (cf. 1 Cor 9:1; 15:8) shattered his earlier identity. It convinced him that the Christians were right and thus that the direction of his life, culminating in persecution of Christians, was wrong (cf. 1 Cor 15:9; Phil 3:7-8). But in the ruins of this identity Paul found another, that of a follower and apostle of Jesus. This second identity was also supported by an identification with God, but now a conscious identification with God as revealed in Jesus. This identity did not allow the direct expression of Paul's competitive character, but was in conflict with it since Paul now understood himself as entirely dependent upon God. However, despite the conflict it created, his new identity suited him, perhaps because it restrained his competitive character from possible excesses (such as persecution) while allowing its controlled expression through the identification of his striving with the action of God in him.

Notes

[1]Or at least this is how Paul saw himself at the time he wrote. For a discussion of the way the retrospective point of view influences Paul and Augustine, see P. Fredriksen, "Paul and Augustine: Conversion Narratives, Orthodox Traditions, and the Retrospective Self," JTS 37 (1986) 3-34.

[2]According to B. Gaventa, 'a Hebrew of the Hebrews' is generally interpreted to mean one of three things: a) Paul and his family were Jewish rather than Gentile, b) they spoke Aramaic or Hebrew, or c) they were not Hellenized but used Jewish language and customs. Gaventa argues that 'b' is most likely (B. Gaventa, Paul's Conversion: A Critical Sifting of the Epistolary Evidence [Duke University dissertation, 1978] 270-72).

[3]As we can see from these passages, comparison of oneself with others is intrinsically competitive; when used positively it is designed to show that one is at least equal to others. Paul seems to show an awareness of this when he recommends in Gal 6:4 that each test his or her own work so as to have a reason to boast in oneself, not another. Likewise in 2 Cor 10:12 Paul says that he will not compare himself with his opponents. But he goes on to criticize them for measuring themselves by themselves and comparing themselves with themselves, which seems to be what he is recommending in Gal 6:4. On the rhetorical use of comparison see H. D. Betz, Der Apostel Paulus und die sokratische Tradition: Eine exegetische Untersuchung zu seiner "Apologie" 2 Korinther 10-13 (BHT 45; Tübingen: Mohr [Siebeck], 1972) 119-20; C. Forbes, "Comparison, Self-Praise and Irony: Paul's Boasting and the Conventions of Hellenistic Rhetoric," NTS 32 (1986) 1-30, especially pp. 2-8. Betz points out that Paul's critique of comparison in 2 Cor 10:12 is similar to the critique of comparison in the popular philosophy of the day (Der Apostel Paulus, 120-21).

[4]A. Stumpff, "zelos ktl.," TDNT 2.877-88.

[5]Ibid. 877-8. In the negative sense zelos is similar in meaning to phthonos.

[6]Ibid. 879, 884.

[7]Ibid. 884; cf. 878.

[8]Ibid. 880-81, 887.

[9]This is commonly recognized as a theme of Paul's theology; cf. R. Bultmann, Theology of the NT (New York: Scribner, 1951, 1955) § 23. In Paul and Palestinian Judaism: A Comparison of Patterns of Religion (Philadelphia: Fortress, 1977) and Paul, the Law and the Jewish People (Philadelphia: Fortress, 1983), E. P. Sanders has argued (correctly, I believe) that Paul's objection to Judaism is most basically that Jews have rejected Christ, not that Judaism essentially entails self-righteousness. However, in making this argument, I think Sanders may underestimate the degree to which Paul retrospectively (perhaps depending excessively on his own experience) analyzes the Jewish failure to believe in Jesus as springing from self-reliance. Of course, Paul is also critical of Gentile self-reliance.

[10]G. Theissen also notes this inconsistency (Psychological Aspects of Pauline Theology trans. by J. P. Galvin [Philadelphia: Fortress, 1987] 34).

[11]In this passage a verb in the first person singular (ekopiasa) is followed by ouk ego...alla. There is a formal parallel to this in 1 Cor 7:10. In Gal 2:20 a verb in the first person singular (zo) is followed by ouketi ego...de. We find another sort of correction in 1 Cor 1:16. All of these may point to differences between Paul's conscious and unconscious attitudes. In each case Paul's first statement would reflect his unconscious attitude and the correction, his conscious attitude. G. Theissen gives a different psychological interpretation of 1 Cor 15:10 and Gal 2:20, seeing them as examples of religious restructuring of causal attribution (Psychological Aspects, 35-6).

[12]On this see W. A. Beardslee, Human Achievement and Divine Vocation in the Message of Paul (SBT 31; Naperville, IL: Allenson, 1961) especially pp. 41-65. That Paul in general allows for human effort by identifying it with the action of God is suggested by 1 Cor 15:58 where Paul urges the Corinthians to abound (perisseuo) in the work of the Lord, knowing that in the Lord their toil is not in vain, and by such descriptions of Christian life as 'walking in the spirit' (Gal 5:16) and 'putting on Christ' (Rom 13:14).

[13]On the theme of identification with Christ see R. Rubenstein, My Brother Paul (New York: Harper and Row, 1972) 23-33.

[14]1 Cor 9:24-7; Gal 2:2; Phil 2:16; 3:14.

[15]V. C. Pfitzner, Paul and the Agon Motif: Traditional Athletic Imagery in the Pauline Literature (NovT Sup 16; Leiden: Brill, 1967) especially pp. 194-5.

[16]Ibid. 16-18; cf. Rom 9:16.

[17]Cf. R. Bultmann's observation that "the hidden side of 'boasting' and 'putting confidence in the flesh' is the fear which the man who is concerned for himself has" (Theology of the NT, 1.243).

[18]Cf. also 1 Cor 11:1; Phil 3:17; and 2 Thess 3:7, 9.

[19]On this topic see W. P. de Boer, The Imitation of Paul: An Exegetical Study (Amsterdam: Kampen, 1962). At the beginning of his study de Boer asks "Can it be that Paul fell victim to the boastful pride which, as Dodd has suggested, was his characteristic temptation?" (p. xi), but he does not explicitly pursue this question. E. Best also raises the question whether or not Paul's presentation of himself as a model involves arrogance, but does not answer it conclusively (Paul and His Converts: The Sprunt Lectures 1985 [Edinburgh: T. & T. Clark, 1988] 8, 59-72).

[20]H. D. Betz, Galatians (Hermeneia; Philadelphia: Fortress, 1979) 86-7.

[21]On this see D. M. Hay, "Paul's Indifference to Authority," JBL 88 (1969) 36-44, especially pp. 39-42.

[22]H. D. Betz, Der Apostel Paulus, 121.

[23]We might think in this connection of the Freudian concepts of reaction-formation, i.e., defense against an undesirable unconscious attitude by adopting the opposite as a conscious attitude, and projection, i.e., defense against an unacceptable unconscious wish or impulse by attributing it to someone else. See C. Brenner, An Elementary Textbook of Psychoanalysis. Revised Edition (Garden City, NY: Doubleday, 1974) 84-8, 91-3. Jungian psychology also speaks of projection; see M. A. Mattoon, Jungian Psychology in Perspective (New York: Free Press, 1981) 126-33.

[24]On Paul's view of boasting see R. Bultmann, "kauchaomai ktl.," TDNT 3.648-52; J. Sánchez Bosch, "Gloriarse" segun San Pablo: Sentido y teologia de kauchaomai (AnBib 40 and Colectanea San Paciano, 16; Rome: Biblical Institute/Barcelona: Facultad de Teologia (SSP), 1970), helpfully reviewed by R. J. Karris, JBL 92 (1973) 144-6.
    Boasting is widely recognized as an important topic in Paul's letters. Many, like Bultmann, argue that Paul has developed a distinctive view of boasting which he maintains consistently. Others, like Betz, argue that Paul reflects attitudes toward boasting which were common in his day. In what follows I argue that both are true. I suggest that Paul both shared the attitudes toward boasting which were common in his day and developed a distinctive view of boasting. In my view, Paul did not fully reconcile the two.

[25]This same tension can be seen in Paul's references to honor and shame. In 1 Thess 2:6 Paul says that when he was with the Thessalonians he did not seek glory (doxan) from human beings, either from them or from others. But then he says in v 20 that they are his glory. Similarly, in 2 Cor 10:15 Paul expresses the hope that the Corinthians will praise him (megalynthenai) abundantly. And in Rom 15:20 Paul says that he makes it a point of honor (philotimoumenon) to preach the gospel where Christ has not been named.

Paul's continuing concern for honor appears even more clearly, though indirectly, in his references to shame. (He mentions both in 2 Cor 6:8). Twice he refers to his shame (atimia) with a heavy irony which implies that it is not shame at all (1 Cor 4:10; 2 Cor 11:21). Elsewhere he says that he has renounced the hidden things of shame (aischynes 2 Cor 4:2), and that he was not put to shame (kateschynthen 2 Cor 7:14), denies that he is ashamed (epaischynomai Rom 1:16; cf. 2 Tim 1:12), and says that he will not be put to shame (aischynomai 2 Cor 10:8; Phil 1:20). In 2 Cor 9:4 he asks the Corinthians not to behave in such a way that he will be put to shame (kataischynthomen).

Likewise Paul urges his readers to seek honor and avoid shame. He tells the Thessalonians that each should possess his vessel in holiness and honor (time 1 Thess 4:4), and that they should make it a point of honor (philotimeisthai) to live quietly (v 11). To the Corinthians he says that we make it a point of honor (philotimoumetha) to be well-pleasing to God (2 Cor 5:9). In 1 Cor 11:22 Paul accuses some of the Corinthians of putting poorer members of the congregation to shame (kataischyno); in 14:35 he says that it is shameful (aischros) for a woman to speak in church. Paul also implies that shame is to be avoided in Rom 6:21; Phil 3:19; cf. Eph 5:4, 12; Titus 1:11.

This concern is especially prominent in 1 Cor 11:2-16 where Paul discusses head coverings for men and women largely in terms of what is shameful (v 4, 5, 6), fitting (prepon v 13), dishonorable (atimia v 14) or glorious (doxa v 15). Cf. also 1 Cor 12:23-4; and cf. 2 Tim 2:20-21.

On Paul's use of the language of honor and shame in Romans see H. Moxnes, "Honor, Shame, and the Outside World in Paul's Letter to the Romans," The Social World of Formative Christianity and Judaism: Essays in Tribute to Howard Clark Kee ed. by J. Neusner et al. (Philadelphia: Fortress, 1988) 207-18.

Another reflection of Paul's inconsistency with regard to boasting can be seen in his treatment of

humility as negative in some passages (e.g., 2 Cor
10:1) and positive in others (e.g., Phil 2:3). On this
see K. Wengst, Humility: Solidarity of the Humiliated.
The Transformation of an Attitude and its Social
Relevance in Graeco-Roman, Old Testament-Jewish and
Early Christian Tradition trans. by J. Bowden
(Philadelphia: Fortress, 1988) 45-53.

[26]On this passage see J. Lambrecht, "Why Is
Boasting Excluded? A Note on Rom 3:27 and 4:2," ETL 61
(1985) 365-9; R. W. Thompson, "Paul's Double Critique
of Jewish Boasting: A Study of Rom 3,27 in Its
Context," Bib 67 (1986) 520-31.
    B. R. Gaventa ("'Where Then Is Boasting?': Romans
3:27 and Its Contexts," Proceedings of the Eastern
Great Lakes Biblical Society 5 (1985) 57-66) argues
that in Rom 3:27 Paul rejects only boasting in one's
special status as a Jew, not boasting as such. While
this is true, when this passage is taken together with
others in which Paul criticizes boasting, especially 1
Cor 1:26-31, the net effect seems to be rejection of
any boasting about oneself.
    H. Hübner ("Boasting and Refraining from
Boasting," Law in Paul's Thought trans. by J. C. G.
Greig [Edinburgh: T. & T. Clark, 1984] 101-24) argues
that in Gal 6:4 "Paul does recognize a genuine claim on
the part of the Christian to 'glory' on the basis of
his life's work" (p 108) and that it is only in Rom 4:2
that Paul excludes this (see especially p 119).
However, Hübner can take this position only by arguing
that Gal 6:13-14 has nothing in common with v 4 except
'glorying' as such (p 111). By contrast I see Gal
6:13-14 as an anticipation of Paul's exclusion of any
boasting about one's accomplishments, though this is
not explicit in the passage; and v 4 is a reflection
of the unconscious persistence of boasting in Paul
despite his conscious opposition to it.

[27]Bultmann, "kauchaomai," 650-51.

[28]Bultmann is aware that Paul could justify
boasting in this way ("kauchaomai," 649), but does not
appeal to it as an explanation of Paul's boasting in
general, perhaps because he has not seen the extent to
which Paul is a competitor. He does recognize the
competitive character of Paul's boasting in 2 Cor 10-
13, however (Ibid. 652). H. D. Betz seems to deny the
competitive character of the boasting in 2 Cor 10-13;
his arguments will be noted below.

[29]This polemic against boasting is also reflected in Paul's criticism of the Corinthians for being puffed up (physioo - 1 Cor 4:6, 18, 19; 5:2; 8:1; 13:4).

[30]E. Käsemann ("A Pauline Version of the 'Amor Fati,'" NT Questions of Today trans. by W. J. Montague [Philadelphia: Fortress, 1969] 217-35) perceives the possibility that in 1 Cor 9:15-18 Paul is inconsistent with his own critique of boasting (pp. 219-22) and attempts to eliminate the inconsistency by seeing Paul's renunciation of financial support as proceeding from necessity (anagke pp. 228-35). In this he has been followed by H. Conzelmann, 1 Corinthians trans. by J. W. Leitch (Hermeneia; Philadelphia: Fortress, 1975) 157-8. However, this interpretation does not seem to do justice to Paul's distinction between preaching the gospel itself and preaching it free of charge.
C. K. Barrett (The First Epistle to the Corinthians [New York: Harper and Row, 1968] 209) and more recently R. F. Hock (The Social Context of Paul's Ministry: Tentmaking and Apostleship [Philadelphia: Fortress, 1980] 62) have suggested that in 1 Cor 9:15-18 Paul is boasting in weakness. That Paul could have regarded this as boasting in weakness is clear from his equation of preaching the gospel without charge to self-abasement in 2 Cor 11:7. However, Paul does not sound like he is boasting in weakness in 1 Cor 9:15-18, and Hock himself has described the Cynic ideal (pp. 39-41) which Paul might here boast that he fulfills. G. Theissen, who has proposed an extremely interesting interpretation of Paul's discussion of self-support here and elsewhere in 1 and 2 Corinthians ("Legitimation and Subsistence: An Essay on the Sociology of Early Christian Missionaries," The Social Setting of Pauline Christianity trans. by J. H. Schütz [Philadelphia: Fortress, 1982] 27-67), also describes this Cynic ideal (pp. 39-40). Likewise J. T. Fitzgerald has argued that the peristasis catalogue in 1 Cor 4:9-13, which includes Paul's working with his own hands (v 12), is used to show how God exhibits Paul as a model in and through his hardships, much as others used such catalogues to make a similar point about the sage (Cracks in an Earthen Vessel: An Examination of the Catalogues of Hardships in the Corinthian Correspondence [SBLDS 99; Atlanta: Scholars, 1988] 117-48, especially pp. 147-8). It seems that Paul could regard his manual labor as an example of either weakness or strength and that in 1 Cor 9:15-18 he boasts of it as the latter. For this view see C. H. Dodd, "The Mind of Paul I," NT Studies (Manchester:

University Press, 1953) 79-80. Note that Paul seems to have little interest in 2 Cor 11:7-10 in the idea that preaching the gospel free of charge was self-abasement (this may be the view of his opponents, though Paul does not reject it); rather Paul discusses it as a matter of refraining from burdening the Corinthians, i.e., strength.

[31]For a detailed proposal as to how such comparison may have arisen see N. A. Dahl, "Paul and the Church at Corinth According to 1 Corinthians 1:10-4:21," Studies in Paul (Minneapolis: Augsburg, 1977) 40-61, especially pp. 45-52.

[32]That this is so receives some support from 2 Cor 3:1 and 5:12 where Paul seems to be responding to a charge that he recommended himself to the Corinthians (cf. also 2 Cor 4:5). The Corinthians may have defended their unfavorable assessment of Paul by saying that he commended himself while his rivals were commended by others, or that his self-commendation was less impressive than that of the rivals. Implicitly in 3:1 and explicitly in 5:12 Paul denies that he is commending himself (cf. also 4:5) and in 2 Cor 10:12 and 18 he criticizes those who commend themselves. But as is the case with boasting, so also in the case of self-commendation; even as Paul denies that he commends himself and condemns it, he also commends himself in 2 Cor 4:2 and in 6:4 as a servant of the Lord. This suggests that the Corinthians may have been correct in saying that Paul commended himself.
      Similarly, in Gal 1:10 Paul implicitly denies that he is persuading men or pleasing them (on this passage see Betz, Galatians, 54-6), and he explicitly denies the latter in 1 Thess 2:4 (cf. Col 3:22; Eph 6:6). Yet he can say in 1 Cor 10:33 that he tries to please all men, and in 2 Cor 5:11 that he persuades men.

[33]Cf. 2 Cor 1:14; 7:4, 14; 8:24; 9:2, 3.

[34]S. N. Olson, Confidence Expressions in Paul: Epistolary Conventions and the Purpose of 2 Corinthians (Yale University dissertation, 1976) 59. See now S. N. Olson, "Pauline Expressions of Confidence in His Addressees," CBQ 47 (1985) 282-95; and cf. "Epistolary Uses of Expressions of Self-Confidence," JBL 103 (1984) 585-97. In an excursus in his dissertation Olson argues that at least 2 Corinthians 1-8 or 9 form an original unity (Confidence Expressions in Paul, 206-15). In what follows I prescind from any discussion of

the integrity of 2 Corinthians because my argument is compatible with any of the common theories about this.

[35]For a detailed account of the situation in Corinth which forces Paul into this contradiction see J. H. Schütz, Paul and the Anatomy of Apostolic Authority (SNTSMS 26; Cambridge: University Press, 1975) 165-86, especially pp. 183-6.

[36]Cf. 2 Cor 11:1, 16-19, 21, 23; 12:11; also 12:1. H. D. Betz (Der Apostel Paulus, 70-100) argues that the boasting which is part of Paul's 'foolish discourse' (2 Cor 11:1 or 16 to 12:13) is consciously used by Paul as part of a reductio ad absurdam of the boasting of his rivals and so is not inconsistent with Paul's argument that proper boasting is boasting in weakness. Even if this is so, it seems psychologically significant that Paul's style of argument here allows him to boast of his achievements even as he renounces them as a proper basis for boasting. Gal 1:13-16 and Phil 3:3-11 may be other examples of the same thing.

[37]According to p[46] and Codexes Sinaiticus and Vaticanus, in 2 Cor 5:12 Paul says that he is trying to give the Corinthians cause to boast about themselves. This reading is accepted by J. -F. Collange, Enigmes de la Deuxieme Epitre de Paul aux Corinthians. Etude Exegetique de 2 Cor 2:14-7:4 (Cambridge: University Press, 1972) 247-8.   If this reading is correct, then Paul does not contradict himself in 2 Cor 5:12.   R. Bultmann   ("Exegetische   Probleme   des   2. Korintherbriefes," Exegetica. Aufsätze zur Erforschung des NT ed. by E. Dinkler [Tübingen: Mohr (Siebeck), 1967] 307-8) eliminates contradiction by interpreting the verse to mean that Paul is not trying to give the Corinthians reason to boast in appearance, but in something invisible.   In this he has been followed by V. P. Furnish, II Corinthians (AB 32A; Garden City, NY: Doubleday, 1984) 323-4.   To me it seems likely that Paul here speaks of giving the Corinthians reason to boast in his appearance so that they will have something to oppose to those who boast in appearance.

[38]E. Käsemann ("Die Legitimät des Apostels. Eine Untersuchung zu II Korinther 10-13," ZNW 41 (1942) 33-71) has argued that the superlative apostles are the "Urapostel," not Paul's opponents in Corinth (pp. 41-8).   In this he has been followed by C. K. Barrett, The Second Epistle to the Corinthians (New York: Harper and Row, 1973) 277-9.   This argument has been

adequately refuted by Bultmann ("Exegetische Probleme,"
318-20); see now Furnish, II Corinthians, 502-5.

[39]If Paul accuses his opponents of measuring
themselves by themselves here, then he seems to be
contradicting his implied rejection of comparing
oneself with others in 2 Cor 10:12 (cf. also Gal 6:4).
According to D* and G Paul says that because he
measures himself by himself, he avoids boasting without
limit. This may be a correction. For an argument in
support of the longer text see Furnish, II Corinthians,
470-71.

[40]In Paul's other reference to his practice of
confining his missionary activity to places where the
gospel has not previously been preached, i.e., Rom
15:20-22, Paul cites Is 52:15 in support of this
policy. His belief that this passage applies to him
may explain what Paul has in mind when he says that God
established the measure of the limit according to which
he boasts (2 Cor 10:13). This is the view of T. Holtz,
"Zum Selbstverständnis des Apostels Paulus," TLZ 91
(1966) 327.

[41]H. D. Betz (Der Apostel Paulus, 97) considers
this a parody of the topos peri eugeneias, though he
gives no particularly convincing reasons and seems to
presuppose that Paul cannot consider this a serious
ground for boasting. This may be partly because Betz
sees Paul as consistent in his position on boasting and
does not consider the possibility that Paul's
competitive character reasserts itself in the face of
his conscious attitude toward boasting.

[42]H. D. Betz (Ibid., 84-93; see also "Eine
Christus-Aretalogie bei Paulus," ZThK 66 [1969] 288-
305) argues that Paul here parodies an ascension
narrative and a healing miracle. Even if this is so,
Paul may still be mentioning what is in some sense for
him a real ground for boasting even as he rejects the
boast. V. P. Furnish concedes that Paul is parodying
an ascension narrative (II Corinthians, 543), but
denies that he parodies a healing miracle (Ibid. 547).

[43]J. T. Fitzgerald has convincingly shown that
boasting about hardship, especially in connection with
peristasis catalogues, is very common in the ancient
world, and that there is even precedent for viewing
victory over hardship as made possible by the divine
(Cracks in an Earthen Vessel, 107-14). 2 Cor 4:7-11

seems to be an example of this in Paul, as Fitzgerald argues (Ibid. 166-7, 170-72). However, by speaking of boasting in weakness as he does in 2 Cor 11:30; 12:5, 9-10, Paul at least heightens the paradox involved in such boasting. To speak of boasting in weakness shifts the focus of attention from overcoming hardship to the hardship itself, and claims success not in spite of the weakness, but somehow within the weakness.

[44]C. H. Dodd ("The Mind of Paul I," 79-81) also notes that even after his conversion Paul continues to boast. Dodd argues that Paul finally gave up boasting at the time of the crisis reflected in 2 Corinthians 10-13. Dodd calls this a second conversion and attempts to show that after this point Paul radically ceased to be "proud, self-assertive and impatient" (Ibid., 81-2) and that Paul's thinking changed with respect to eschatology and universalism ("The Mind of Paul II," NT Studies, 83-128).

As is clear from the foregoing, Dodd considerably simplifies Paul's argument in 2 Corinthians 10-13, overlooking the persistence of straightforward boasting even as Paul develops his new paradoxical understanding of boasting in weakness. Dodd also overlooks Paul's boasting in the letters which, according to Dodd, were written after 2 Corinthians 10-13, e.g., 2 Cor 1:14; 7:4, 14; 8:24; 9:2, 3; Rom 15:17; Phil 2:16. However, it is possible, perhaps even likely, that the new understanding of boasting which Paul develops in 2 Corinthians 10-13 had a lasting effect on him. This may account for the prominence which Paul gives his critique of boasting in Romans (cf. 3:27; 4:2) and his implicit specification of proper boasting as boasting in God (cf. 5:2, 11). Romans also contains Paul's one certain reference to boasting in weakness outside of 2 Corinthians, i.e., Rom 5:3. However, Rom 15:17 makes it clear that Paul has not completely abandoned boasting of his achievements as a servant of Christ.

[45]B. J. Malina, The NT World: Insights from Cultural Anthropology (Atlanta: John Knox, 1981) 25-50. See also his discussion of the relationship between individual and society, pp. 51-60. For Paul's explicit references to honor and shame see note 25 above.

[46]See V. C. Pfitzner, Paul and the Agon Motif; W. P. de Boer, The Imitation of Paul; B. Fiore, The Function of Personal Example in the Socratic and Pastoral Epistles (AnBib 105; Rome: Biblical

Institute, 1986) 33-5, 176-7; and E. Best, <u>Paul</u> <u>and</u> <u>His</u>
<u>Converts</u>, 60-63.   However, Best notes that in
literature apart from Paul's letters, the call to
imitate "is mostly made in the third person...." He
mentions 4 Macc 9:23 and 2 Macc 6:27-8 as exceptions to
this (p. 68).

[47]H. D. Betz, "De Laude Ipsius (Moralia 539 A - 547
F)," <u>Plutarch's</u> <u>Ethical</u> <u>Writings</u> <u>and</u> <u>Early</u> <u>Christian</u>
<u>Literature</u> ed. by H. D. Betz (SCHNT 4; Leiden: Brill,
1978) 367-93.   Earlier Betz argued the same point with
regard to Paul's boasting in 2 Corinthians 10-13,
appealing to Quintilian, <u>Institutio</u> <u>Oratoria</u> 11.1.15-26
in addition to Plutarch's treatise (<u>Der</u> <u>Apostel</u> <u>Paulus</u>,
75-9).   Cf. also E. A. Judge, "Paul's Boasting in
Relation to Contemporary Professional Practice," <u>AusBR</u>
16 (1968) 37-50; C. Forbes, "Comparison, Self-Praise
and Irony."   As we have earlier noted (see n. 30
above), J. T. Fitzgerald has shown the extent to which
even Paul's boasting in weakness conforms to the norms
of his culture.   See also K. Wengst's argument that in
general humility was regarded negatively in Graeco-
Roman culture (<u>Humility</u>, 4-15).

[48]On Greek criticism of boasting see R. Bultmann,
"<u>kauchaomai</u>," <u>TDNT</u> 3.646.

[49]See R. Bultmann, "<u>kauchaomai</u>," <u>TDNT</u> 3.646-8; B.
R. Gaventa, "'Where Then Is Boasting?'" 60-61, 62-4.
See also K. Wengst's argument that humility was
regarded positively in Jewish literature (<u>Humility</u>, 16-
35).

[50]E. H. Erikson, <u>Identity</u> <u>and</u> <u>the</u> <u>Life</u> <u>Cycle</u> (New
York: Norton, 1979) especially pp. 94-100, 118-31.
For a full-scale biographical application of this
theory see E. H. Erikson, <u>Young</u> <u>Man</u> <u>Luther:</u> <u>A</u> <u>Study</u> <u>in</u>
<u>Psychoanalysis</u> <u>and</u> <u>History</u> (New York: Norton, 1958).
    It   is   interesting   to   note   that   there   was
considerable reflection on the life-cycle in antiquity;
see J. LaPorte, "The Ages of Life in Philo of
Alexandria," SBLSP 1986, 278-90.   As might be expected,
ancient understanding of the life-cycle is not very
similar to Erikson's theory in its details.   However,
Philo's description of the fourth age of life, i.e.,
22-28 years, in <u>Heres</u> 298-9 somewhat resembles
Erikson's understanding of the stage of identity.

[51]E. H. Erikson, <u>Identity</u>, 97-8.

Chapter 3

Sexuality

A. Paul's Statements About Sexuality[1]

Paul's references to sexual matters in his letters fall into three groups. The largest consists of condemnations of various kinds of unacceptable sexual behavior. These can be quite general, as in Paul's condemnation of impurity (akatharsia),[2] immorality (porneia)[3] and licentiousness (aselgeia).[4] At other times Paul is more specific about the behavior he condemns: adultery,[5] homosexuality (Rom 1:26-7; 1 Cor 6:9; cf. 1 Tim 1:9-10), covetousness (Rom 7:7-8; 13:9; 1 Thess 4:5), incest (1 Cor 5:1-5) and patronizing prostitutes (1 Cor 6:12-20).

In addition to these frequent condemnations of certain sexual behavior, there are two smaller groups of passages, one which suggests a positive attitude toward sexuality as such, and another expressing a negative attitude. Though it seems fairly clear that Paul's condemnation of sexual sins does not imply a positive attitude toward sexuality in general, it is not yet clear that it implies a negative attitude either. We shall have to return to this question below.

The principal passage in Paul's letters which implies a positive view of sexuality is 1 Cor 6:12-20. In this passage Paul argues against the practice of patronizing prostitutes (v 15-16). The argument is complex. The strand of it which is important for our

purposes is Paul's idea that sexual intercourse with a
prostitute is a blasphemous parody of the relationship
between the believer and Christ. After referring
briefly to his idea that Christians are members of the
body of Christ (cf. 1 Cor 12:12-31; Rom 12:3-8), Paul
asks whether one should make the members of Christ
members of a prostitute (v 15). And he explains that
sexual intercourse with a prostitute makes the two into
one body because that is the essential character of
sexual intercourse; in support of this Paul cites Gen
2:24 (v 16). Though he does not make this explicit,
Paul seems to be relying on the Corinthians to
recognize the inappropriateness of sexual relations
with a prostitute once they realize what is involved.
But the presupposition of the argument is that there is
a parallel or analogy between sexual intercourse and
the union of the believer with Christ. This parallel
makes sexual relations with a prostitute blasphemous.
But we might expect that in other circumstances sexual
intercourse would have a positive value because of this
parallel.

This positive value of sexual intercourse may
appear more directly in 1 Cor 11:2-16 if, as W.. A.
Meeks has argued, Paul is here calling for recognition
of the goodness of God's creation of male and female.[6]
The view that the existence of two sexes is proper
would seem to imply the goodness of sexual intercourse
between them. And in 2 Cor 11:2 Paul says that he has
betrothed the Corinthians to Christ. He uses this
image to exhort them to faithfulness. But it also
seems to imply that Paul sees a parallel between
marriage and the relationship between the believer and
Christ.[7] This parallel is discussed most explicitly in

Eph 5:22-33; this may not have been written by Paul,
but it makes use of the same basic ideas we have seen
in 1 Cor 6:12-20. In this passage the parallel between
marriage and the union of believers with Christ is the
basis for exhortation to husband and wife to relate to
one another as Christ and the church relate to one
another. Once again Gen 2:24 is used to justify the
interpretation of sexual intercourse in the passage.
Both 2 Cor 11:2 and Eph 5:22-33 suggest that it is in
marriage that the parallel between sexual relations and
the union of believers with Christ gives the former a
positive value.[8]

A final passage which may suggest a positive view
of sexuality is 1 Cor 7:7. After expressing a wish
that all might be celibate, Paul says that everyone has
his or her own charism, one of one kind, another of
another. He clearly implies that celibacy is a charism
and contrasts it with other charisms. What is not
clear is whether he implies that marriage is a charism
or is thinking of other, different sorts of gifts which
one might have instead of the gift of celibacy. V 8-9
may seem to make the latter more likely. Still it is
possible that v 7 does imply that marriage is a
charism, and this is certainly the most obvious reading
of the verse in itself.

Alongside these passages which imply a positive
view of sexuality, there are several passages which
seem to express a negative attitude toward sexuality in
general. These are passages in which Paul says that
celibacy is better than marriage and that marriage is a
remedy for sexual immorality.

Most of Paul's expressions of a negative view of
sexuality occur in the course of 1 Corinthians 7; here
again Paul's argument is complex.[9] In 7:1-24 Paul
seems to be agreeing with the ascetical tendency of
some of the Corinthians (v 1 - It is good for a man not
to touch a woman), but also trying to modify it in
order to avoid some of the problems this has caused in
Corinth. In 7:25-40 he discusses virgins in Corinth.
For some reason, with respect to this group the
Corinthian tendency is not toward extreme asceticism,
but rather for these virgins to marry. Paul urges them
to remain unmarried.

In the course of this discussion Paul several
times suggests that marriage is inferior to celibacy.
In v 7 he says, 'I wish all were as I myself am,' i.e.,
celibate (cf. v 8).   This seems to imply the
superiority of celibacy to marriage, a rather dangerous
statement to make in the course of an attempt to
moderate the Corinthians' excessive zeal for celibacy.
But Paul immediately adds that celibacy is a gift from
God (v 7), making it clear that he is urging celibacy
only on those who have received that gift.   Thus in
effect Paul's argument for the superiority of celibacy
is an argument that those who have received this gift
should use it.   Later, as he argues that virgins not
marry, Paul also says that celibacy is the better state
(v 38, 40).

In itself the idea that marriage is inferior to
celibacy is not incompatible with a positive view of
sexuality and marriage. Paul might be thinking that
good as marriage is, celibacy is even better (cf. v
38).   In support of this we might note that Paul

clearly thinks some of the Corinthians have an excessive zeal for celibacy. He warns them that married couples should not cease sexual relations with one another (v 2-7), that single people should not remain single if they do not have the gift of celibacy (v 8-9) and that married couples should not seek divorce (v 10-16). Further, he clearly says that to marry is not a sin (v 28; cf. v 8-9, 36-8, 39).

But in fact Paul does not seem to have, or at least does not express, an understanding of celibacy according to which it is more exalted than marriage. Paul attempts to explain the superiority of celibacy in v 25-35. His basic argument is that celibacy is preferable to marriage because of the present necessity (v 26), i.e., the imminent end of the world (cf. v 29, 31). This makes celibacy preferable to marriage because the latter constitutes involvement with the world which is passing away (v 33-4), involvement which will lead to affliction in the flesh as the world passes away (v 28).[10] However, Paul also uses the imminent end of the world to argue that those who are married should remain married (v 26-7). In addition the married are called to the same detachment from the world as are the unmarried (v 29-31).[11] Thus the imminent end of the world makes celibacy superior to marriage mainly in the sense that it makes Christian detachment from this passing world easier (v 35). This hardly seems to account satisfactorily for Paul's preference for celibacy in itself, and seems to require that he also presuppose a rather negative view of marriage.

If we ask what that understanding is, it seems likely that Paul is thinking that marriage is an outlet for uncontrollable passion. It is because of the danger of sexual immorality, i.e., sexual relations with someone other than one's spouse, that married couples should have sexual relations (v 2, 5), that single people without the gift of celibacy should marry (v 8) and that virgins may marry (v 36-7). This view was probably suggested to Paul by the problems the Corinthians were encountering, but he clearly embraces it himself. According to some interpretations, Paul expresses this same view of marriage in 1 Thess 4:3-5. Here he says that the Thessalonians should avoid immorality (porneia), each holding his vessel (possibly = wife) in holiness and honor.[12]

It is striking that Paul's positive view of sexuality and marriage emerges indirectly, by implication (except in the case of Eph 5:22-33 which may not derive from Paul himself). In 1 Cor 6:12-20 this positive view is implied in the course of an argument against consorting with prostitutes. In 2 Cor 11:2 it is implied as Paul uses sexual infidelity as an image for religious infidelity. By contrast, in 1 Corinthians 7 Paul's negative view of sexuality and marriage is expressed directly. This suggests that the negative view of sexuality and marriage is Paul's most highly conscious one, and that the positive view is less conscious. The latter exists (apart from Ephesians) mainly in the form of ideas about marriage and sexuality which Paul has not yet brought to bear upon explicit discussion of the positive meaning of sexuality and marriage.

Thus far we have seen that in addition to a large number of passages in which Paul condemns unacceptable sexual behavior, there are smaller groups of passage which suggest both a positive and a negative view of sexuality in itself. I have argued that in some passages Paul implicitly views sexual intercourse as establishing a relationship between two people which is analogous to the relationship between Christ and the church. I have also suggested that this view of sexuality is less conscious than is Paul's negative view. The latter is expressed in passages where Paul says that marriage is inferior to celibacy and mainly an outlet for sexual passions when they cannot be controlled. Let us seek further understanding of this split between Paul's conscious and less conscious views of sexuality by locating them in his cultural milieu.

B. **The Cultural Context of Paul's Statements About Sexuality**[13]

Let us first of all consider Paul's condemnation of sexual sins. His general condemnation of impurity (akatharsia), immorality (porneia) and licentiousness (aselgeia) is clearly in accord with his milieu since the words themselves are pejorative. Of course, different opinions were possible about what constituted impurity, immorality and licentiousness. But whatever could be described by those terms was thereby disapproved. When Paul uses these terms, they are often part of a list of vices.[14] Paul's lists are modeled on similar lists used by Hellenistic Jews and Greeks.[15]

It is more informative to consider specific behaviors. In condemning adultery and covetousness Paul is obviously in accord with the Judaism of his day, since these are forbidden by the Ten Commandments (Exod 20:13-17), to which Paul at times explicitly refers (Rom 7:7; 13:9). Adultery is also criticized by Greek and Roman moralists.[16] Paul's condemnation of homosexuality is also in accord with Judaism and with some Greek and Roman moral teaching. However, homosexuality also found acceptance in Greek culture.[17] Similarly Paul's condemnation of incest is in accord with Judaism and with Greek and Roman attitudes.[18] And finally Paul's opposition to patronizing prostitutes echoes Jewish and some Greek and Roman views.[19] This broad agreement between Paul's attitude toward specific sexual behaviors and the attitude found in his milieu, both Jewish and Gentile, suggests that Paul simply repeats the behavioral norms of his culture when he condemns unacceptable sexual behavior.[20] If so, then these condemnations may not inform us about Paul's own attitude toward sexuality except insofar as he participated in the common attitudes of his time.

Paul's implicit positive view of sexuality (i.e., that it establishes a relationship between two people which is analogous to the relationship between Christ and the church) is unique to him. Various elements of this view have parallels elsewhere; however, Paul was probably the first to combine them as he does. This is true first of all with regard to the central image of the body. This image was widely used in Paul's day, especially by the Stoics.[21] However, Paul seems to have been the first to adopt this image and apply it to the Christian church; this conception of the church was a cornerstone of his thinking, as far as we know it.[22] And Paul seems to have been unique in perceiving a parallel between the church, understood in this way, and the union created by sexual intercourse. Thus the view of sexuality which we are considering here is a creative development of one of Paul's central theological insights. 1 Cor 7:7 supplies further confirmation of this if it implies that marriage is a charism. Part of Paul's view of the church as the body of Christ is that the members of the body are given different, mutually interdependent charisms by the spirit (cf. Rom 12:6; 1 Cor 12:4-31). Thus the view that marriage is a gift of the spirit would be another development of Paul's idea that the church is the body of Christ.

Paul's positive view of sexuality is similar to the description of the relationship between God and Israel as a betrothal or marriage in the Hebrew scriptures.[23] However, Paul's idea goes beyond this image in its understanding of the precise similarity between marriage and the relationship of God to Israel. 2 Cor 11:2, which does not specify this similarity, comes closest to the usage of the Hebrew scriptures.

A closer parallel to Paul's understanding of sexuality as something which makes two people one is provided by Plutarch. Probably depending on Stoic ideas, in his Advice to Bride and Groom Plutarch seems to presuppose the view that marriage unites husband and wife into one body. In one place he says that just as blows on the left side (of the body) record the sensation on the right, so it is beautiful for husband and wife to sympathize with one another (20; Moralia

140 E). Later he says that philosophers distinguish
three kinds of bodies (somaton) - those composed of
separate elements, like a fleet, those composed of
elements joined together, like a ship, and those
forming an intimate union, like a living creature. And
he says that marriages are of three corresponding kinds
- those who merely sleep in the same bed are separate
elements; those who marry for dowry or children are
elements joined together; and those who are in love
form an intimate union. Plutarch compares this union
to the mixing of two liquids and says that it should
result in the mutual amalgamation of the bodies,
property, friends and relations of the married couple
(34; Moralia 142 E-F).[24]

This is strikingly similar to Paul's view; both
Plutarch and Paul see sexual relations as making two
people into one body. However, while Paul sees this as
the effect of sexual intercourse in itself, even with a
prostitute, Plutarch sees this as occurring in
marriage, and occurring differently according to the
dispositions of the persons involved. Whatever
contribution ideas such as we see in Plutarch made to
Paul's view, they cannot explain it entirely. But
since Paul appeals directly to Gen 2:24 in 1 Cor 6:16,
and the same passage is cited in Eph 5:31, it seems
likely that this passage lies at the root of Paul's
understanding of sexuality as something which makes two
people one.

Such an understanding of sexuality might seem to
flow rather directly from the passage itself; after all
it does say that husband and wife become one flesh.
There are some indications that this is how the passage

was understood by other Jews of Paul's day. In L. A.
2.49-52 Philo interprets Gen 2:24 as speaking about
unity, but he takes it as an allegory of the unity of
mind (= man) with sense perception (= woman). And he
understands their becoming flesh as meaning a descent
to an inferior level of being (cf. Gig. 65). In Q Gen.
1.29 he interprets the passage along the same lines,
but literally, as applying to husband and wife. He
says that the verse commands husband to act toward his
wife with the most extreme exaggeration in partnership.
Their union in one flesh

> indicates something very tangible and sense-
> perceptible, in which there is suffering and
> sensual pleasure, that they may rejoice in,
> and be pained by, and feel the same things,
> and much more, may think the same things.

Philo does understand the verse as speaking about
unity, but as applied to literal husband and wife it is
a unity which is commanded, not created by sexual
intercourse.

Rabbinic interpretation of Gen 2:24 (coming from
long after the time of Paul, but perhaps reflecting
ideas already known in his day) also takes Gen 2:24 as
implying commands. For example, we find in b. Sanh.
58a

> It has been taught: Therefore shall a man
> leave his father and his mother; R. Eliezer
> said: His father means 'his father's
> sister;' his mother, 'his mother's sister.'
> R. Akiba said: His father means 'his
> father's wife;' his mother is literally
> meant. And he shall cleave, but not to a
> male; to his wife, but not to his neighbor's
> wife; and they shall be as one flesh,
> applying to those that can become one flesh,
> thus excluding cattle and beasts, which
> cannot become one flesh with man.[25]

This type of interpretation takes the verse as implying

the nature of the proper partner in marriage and sexual intercourse. There is an interpretation closer to that of Paul in Gen. Rab. 18.5 where it says that among the Gentiles sexual intercourse acquires, i.e., creates a union between man and woman. The same thing is said more generally (but without specific reference to Gen 2:24) in m. Qidd. 1.1 where sexual intercourse is identified as one of the things which acquire, along with money and document (cf. m. Ket. 4.4).

Paul's interpretation of Gen 2:24 may presuppose that human beings were originally created masculofeminine (Gen 1:27) and were subsequently separated into males and females (Gen 2:21-2); thus sexual intercourse unites male and female into one body, restoring the original unity of creation (Gen 2:24). Other Jews, adapting Greek views, explicitly interpreted Genesis as describing a first, bisexual creation followed by separation of human beings into two sexes. W. A. Meeks argues that these ideas underlie Gal 3:28.[26] The earliest explicit interpretation of Gen 2:24 along these lines is found in a saying of Jesus. According to Mark 10:6-9/Matt 19:4-6 Jesus appealed to Gen 1:27 and 2:24 as showing that sexual intercourse in marriage restores the original unity of creation, and thus that marriage is indissoluble.[27] This suggests the possibility that Paul's understanding of Gen 2:24 and of sexuality derives from specifically Christian tradition, perhaps going back to Jesus himself. The view that marriage restores the original unity of creation is also explicit in the later rabbinic literature. For example, in b. Yebam. 63a it says that one who has no wife is not a human being; this is supported by a reference to Gen 5:2, which recapitulates Gen 1:27. (Cf. also Gen. Rab. 17.2; Qoh. Rab. 9.9).

What of Paul's negative view of sexuality (i.e., that marriage is inferior to celibacy and chiefly a remedy for sexual immorality)? Like his positive view, this seems unique to Paul; however, elements of his attitude do have parallels elsewhere. Although Judaism regarded marriage as a duty and for Greeks marriage was the normal thing,[28] there were some Jews and even more Greeks who regarded celibacy as preferable to marriage. Among the Jews at least some of the Essenes were said to practice celibacy (Josephus, J. W. 2.120; Ant. 18.21). Among the Greeks it was widely held that sexual relations involved loss of the vital spirit in the seed. Thus sexual relations had a harmful effect on a person, and sexual abstinence was desirable. We find this view expressed particularly in medical literature.[29] In addition the Epicureans, Cynics and Neoplatonists all favored celibacy over marriage.[30]

It seems possible that Paul's preference for celibacy owes something to the view that sexual intercourse is harmful, but he gives no direct indication that it does. The Epicureans' inclination toward sexual abstinence seems to have been based on the view that the satisfaction of sexual desire is not necessary; and instead of quenching desire, attempting to satisfy sexual desire increases it. Thus sexual pleasure is accompanied by pain.[31] However, their avoidance of marriage was not absolute; the wise person might marry because of special circumstances (Diogenes Laertius, Lives 10.118-19). Closer to Paul is the celibacy of the Cynic. According to Epictetus, the

Cynic avoided marriage because of his social role in present circumstances, which are equivalent to conditions of war (Epictetus 3.22.67-76, especially 69, 76). This sort of view might readily account for the celibacy of the apostle, but would not so well account for Paul's advocacy of celibacy for all Christians.[32] The closest parallel to Paul's position is provided by those Essenes who were celibate. They seem to have undertaken celibacy in fulfillment of the requirements for holy war (cf. Deut 23:9-11; 2 Sam 11:9-13).[33] They held themselves in readiness for participation in the eschatological battle, which would be a holy war. This is similar to Paul's position in advocating celibacy on eschatological grounds; however, Paul does not seem to have the ideology of holy war in mind. And as we have seen, Paul's appeal to eschatology is combined with a negative view of marriage. This was not the case for the Essenes.

Paul's view that marriage is a remedy for sexual immorality also has parallels in his environment. Most of all it is reminiscent of Jewish statements about marrying so as to avoid sin. For example, in T. Levi 9.9-10 Isaac tells Levi to take a wife while he is young so as to avoid sexual immorality.[34] However, despite the similarity between Paul's view and passages such as this, there is also an important difference between them. Other Jews speak of marrying to avoid sin in the context of a presumption that virtually all will marry, in obedience to the command of God. In this context the avoidance of sexual immorality is just one of the reasons for marrying, and a subordinate one at that. But in 1 Corinthians 7 Paul speaks of marrying to avoid sexual immorality in the context of

choosing between marriage and celibacy. Because Paul
contemplates celibacy as a possibility, the idea of
marrying to avoid immorality becomes a more central
definition of the purpose of marriage for Paul than for
other Jews. On the other hand, even as Paul makes
avoidance of immorality a central purpose of marriage,
his concern with the former does not lead him to
counsel avoidance of contact with women; similar
concern does lead many other Jews to advise this.[35]

Among both Jews and Greeks procreation is seen as
the primary purpose of marriage;[36] and some writers
such as Musonius Rufus also emphasize community of life
between husband and wife as a purpose of marriage.[37]
Paul may not consider procreation the purpose of
marriage because of his expectation of the imminent end
of the world.[38] And at the same time he avoids the
consequence of an extreme emphasis on procreation found
in some contemporary writers, i.e., the view that even
in marriage sexual indulgence apart from procreation is
undesirable.[39]

Thus we see that both Paul's positive view and his
negative view of sexuality have parallels in his
cultural environment. We have seen that the positive
view takes over an understanding of Gen 2:24 according
to which sexuality is something that makes man and
woman one; it also rests on use of the image of the
body. However, Paul was the first to apply this image
to the church and the first to see a parallel between
the church, understood in this way, and sexual union.
Thus this positive view, despite its points of contact
with Paul's cultural milieu, can be seen as a creative
development of Paul's own thought.

At first glance it might seem that Paul's negative view of sexuality derives more straightforwardly from his culture. As we have seen, a preference for celibacy and the view that marriage is a remedy for sexual immorality are not at all unique to Paul. However, Paul's reasons for advocating celibacy for all Christians do not fully correspond to the reasons for which others advocated celibacy in his day. Like some of the Essenes Paul advocates celibacy on eschatological grounds. But Paul's appeal to eschatology is not the same as that of the Essenes; and in fact his appeal to eschatology does not seem to account fully for his preference for celibacy. The latter is also based on an understanding of marriage as principally an outlet for uncontrollable sexual desire. Although such a view of marriage is not unique to Paul, he is unique in making it a definition of the purpose of marriage. Thus Paul's negative view of sexuality and marriage, despite its points of contact with his culture, is also particular to Paul.

C. Psychological Analysis of Paul's Statements About Sexuality

The picture which emerges from all of this is that in addition to adopting from his culture its estimate of proper and improper sexual behavior, Paul also had a consciously negative attitude toward sexuality and a less conscious, implicit, positive attitude toward it. Both of these attitudes also had points of contact with Paul's culture, but both were particular to Paul in the way he expressed them. Both attitudes were congenial to Paul's Christian identity. But as we have seen,

Paul's positive attitude seems to flow directly from his Christian faith, while his negative attitude does not. Paul appeals to his eschatological expectations in support of his preference for celibacy. But the appeal does not seem to account for the preference entirely; in part it is a rationalization of a preference which has its origin elsewhere.

This suggests that before he became a Christian Paul had a negative attitude toward sexuality and that it was becoming a Christian which fostered the growth in him of a positive attitude toward sexuality. However, Paul may never have embraced this view with full consciousness; and his earlier view persisted and comes to expression as he discusses various questions in his letters. It accords well with this that Paul most often mentions sexual matters in condemning unacceptable sexual behavior.

I have suggested that becoming a Christian fostered a positive attitude toward sexuality on Paul's part. It would be more accurate to say that becoming a Christian fostered the conscious acceptance of a positive attitude. Given the nature of the sexual appetite, at some level Paul must always have viewed its satisfaction positively. In fact this also emerges indirectly from the negative attitude itself. Paul preferred celibacy to marriage, seeing the latter as an outlet for uncontrollable sexual desire. This view suggests that at some level of his personality Paul was drawn to the fulfillment of sexual desire. If in Rom 7:7-8 'You shall not covet' refers to sexual covetousness, and if this passage has an oblique autobiographical reference,[40] then it indicates directly the existence of this attitude in Paul.

Before he became a Christian Paul consciously rejected this attraction. He considered that it was best to suppress it, or if that was not possible, to channel it into marriage. Even after he became a Christian, this remained Paul's conscious attitude.[41] In fact, becoming a Christian reinforced this attitude in more than one way. First, as a Christian Paul was called to be an apostle, a vocation for which celibacy was suitable, as it was for the Cynic philosopher. Second, as a Christian he expected the end of the world soon, a situation which also encouraged celibacy, since it eliminated procreation as a purpose for marriage and made celibacy practically advantageous in various ways. But becoming a Christian also allowed Paul to embrace a more positive attitude toward sexuality as Paul moved toward seeing sexual union in marriage as an analogue of the union of believers with Christ.

This analysis leaves us with at least two questions: why did Paul have a consciously negative attitude toward sexuality? and how did becoming a Christian foster his acceptance of a positive attitude? Any answer must be speculative, since there is no relevant data. I will offer two such speculations.

First, as we have noted, Paul's preference for celibacy may have been based on the idea that sexual intercourse is harmful, involving the loss of vital spirit. If so, it is possible that seeing Jesus, who emptied himself (Phil 2:7), as a model may have weakened resistance to this loss of self and allowed the development of a more positive attitude toward it.

Whatever may be the merits of this suggestion, it answers our questions mainly in cognitive terms and does not address the underlying psychological dynamics. For an answer to the questions which does do this, we can turn to the theory of the Oedipus complex.[42] According to psychoanalytic theory, roughly between the ages of three and six years every person is attracted to his or her parent of the opposite sex (mainly) and wishes to eliminate the parent of his or her own sex, but fears the retaliation of the latter as well as the loss of that parent's love.[43] The usual resolution of the Oedipus complex is that the child partly abandons, partly represses his or her incestuous wishes[44] and does so by identifying with the parent of his or her own sex (primarily), internalizing this parent's opposition to those wishes. This internalization of the parent's opposition to the incestuous wishes is the effective beginning of the superego.[45] In support of the superego's prohibition of sexuality the ego makes use of various defenses against sexual impulses, including reaction-formation, i.e., adoption of a conscious negative attitude toward sexuality to counteract the unconscious inclination toward it.[46]

In these terms we can explain Paul's preference for celibacy and his view of sexuality as a threat to this preference, as partly the result of an unusually strong prohibition of sexuality on the part of his superego and the existence in him of an unusually strong reaction-formation against it. This could have resulted either from the severity of his father, with whom he identified in resolving the Oedipus complex, or from the strength of his own desire to eliminate his father, which he then turned against himself in identifying with his father.[47]

Paul's later life would then have modified his superego by means of identifications subsequent to the original identification with his father.[48] As we have seen, it seems likely that before his conversion Paul unconsciously identified himself with God, seeking to excel in the service of God. This identification may have mainly reinforced Paul's original identification with his father. But as a result of his conversion Paul consciously identified with Jesus and with God as revealed in Jesus. As S. Tarachow has suggested, this identification, particularly with Jesus, the son, may have symbolized for Paul overcoming, rather than submitting to his father.[49] If so, then Paul's conversion may have modified his superego, making it less harsh in its prohibition of sexuality than before, and opening the door to Paul's adoption of a more positive attitude toward sexuality.

An explanation of Paul's statements about sexuality in terms of the Oedipus complex is extremely speculative. But it does offer a satisfying explanation in terms which are widely accorded at least some validity. Further investigation may help to refine this hypothesis.

Notes

[1]For a recent discussion of Paul's view of sexuality in terms that differ from, but are congenial to what follows, see P. Brown, The Body and Society: Men, Women and Sexual Renunciation in Early Christianity (Lectures on the History of Religions, new

series, 13; New York: Columbia University Press, 1988)
46-57.

[2]Rom 1:24; 6:19; 2 Cor 6:17; 12:21; 'Gal 5:19; 1
Thess 2:3; 4:7; cf. Eph 4:17-19; 5:3, 5; Col 3:5.

[3]1 Cor 5:9-11; 6:9; 10:8; 2 Cor 12:21; Gal 5:19; 1
Thess 4:3; cf. Eph 5:3, 5; Col 3:5; 1 Tim 1:9-10.

[4]Rom 13:13; 2 Cor 12:21; Gal 5:19; cf. Eph 4:17-
19.

[5]Rom 2:22; 7:3-4; 13:9; 1 Cor 6:9.

[6]W. A. Meeks, "The Image of the Androgyne: Some
Uses of a Symbol in Earliest Christianity," HR 13
(1973-4) 200-203. For a more recent discussion of this
passage, which sums up the abundant recent literature
on it, see D. R. MacDonald, "Ritual, Sex and Veils at
Corinth," There Is No Male and Female: The Fate of a
Dominical Saying in Paul and Gnosticism (HDR 20;
Philadelphia: Fortress, 1987) 65-111.   Like Meeks,
MacDonald sees Paul as affirming the goodness of the
existence of two genders, male and female (see
especially pp. 108-10).

[7]On this passage see R. A. Batey, "Paul's Bride
Image.   A Symbol of Realistic Eschatology," Int 17
(1963) 176-82; NT Nuptial Imagery (Leiden: Brill,
1971) 12-19.   Batey considers, but rejects, the
possibility that this same image is used in Rom 7:1-6.

[8]On Eph 5:22-33 see R. Batey, "The MIA SARX Union
of Christ and the Church," NTS 13 (1967) 270-81; NT
Nuptial Imagery, 20-37; J. P. Sampley, 'And the Two
Shall Become One Flesh': A Study of Traditions in
Ephesians 5:21-33 (SNTSMS 16; Cambridge: University
Press, 1971).

[9]For a recent and thorough discussion of this
passage, see O. L. Yarbrough, Not Like the Gentiles:
Marriage Rules in the Letters of Paul (SBLDS 80;
Atlanta: Scholars, 1985) 93-117; V. L. Wimbush, Paul
the Worldly Ascetic: Response to the World and Self-
Understanding according to 1 Corinthians 7 (Macon, GA:
Mercer, 1987).

[10]Yarbrough (Not Like the Gentiles, 103-4) sees v
32-5 as indicating a second reason, in addition to
eschatological expectation, for the superiority of

celibacy.   Yarbrough sums up this reason as "the mission of believers" (p 104).   One problem with this is that 'mission of believers' is not obviously appropriate to describe what celibacy allows, i.e., pleasing the Lord (v 32), being holy (v 34), good order and devotion to the Lord (v 35).   But more importantly, Paul's statement that marriage involves being anxious about the things of the world (v 33-4) links this section with the previous discussion of involvement with the world which is passing away (v 31).   On this see Wimbush, Paul the Worldly Ascetic, 49-71.

[11]On this passage see Wimbush, Paul the Worldly Ascetic, 23-47.

[12]For a detailed argument that Paul is here urging marriage so as to avoid immorality, see Yarbrough, Not Like the Gentiles, 68-76.

[13]The most extensive treatment of sexuality in the Greco-Roman world is that of M. Foucault, The History of Sexuality, trans. by R. Hurley. Vol. 2, The Use of Pleasure (New York: Pantheon, 1985) discusses the way sexuality was problematized in the classical Greek culture of the 4th century BCE; vol. 3, The Care of the Self (New York: Pantheon, 1986) discusses the same problematization in the Greek and Latin texts of the first two centuries of our era.   Brown discusses sexuality among Jews as well as Gentiles in The Body and Society, 5-40.   For a recent discussion of this subject which pays special attention to points of contact with Paul, see Yarbrough, Not Like the Gentiles, 7-63.

[14]Cf. Rom 13:13; 1 Cor 5:10-11; 6:9-10; 2 Cor 12:20-21; Gal 5:19-21; and Eph 5:3-5; Col 3:5; 1 Tim 1:9-10.

[15]H. Conzelmann, 1 Corinthians trans. by J. W. Leitch (Hermeneia; Philadelphia: Fortress, 1975) 100-101.

[16]On this see Yarbrough, Not Like the Gentiles, 57-60; Foucault, The Use of Pleasure, 145-51; The Care of the Self, 165-75.   For a detailed discussion of Roman law concerning adultery see A. Rousselle, Porneia: On Desire and the Body in Antiquity, trans. by F. Pheasant (Family, Sexuality, and Social Relations in Past Times; New York: Blackwell, 1988) 78-92.   In these pages

Rousselle also refers to the prohibition of incest and stuprum by Roman law.

[17]Conzelmann, 1 Corinthians, 106-7. For a detailed discussion of divided opinion among Greeks and Romans concerning homosexuality, and of Jewish opposition to it, see R. Scroggs, The NT and Homosexuality: Contextual Background for Contemporary Debate (Philadelphia: Fortress, 1983) 17-98, especially pp. 44-98. On Greek and Roman views see also Foucault, The Use of Pleasure, 187-246; The Care of the Self, 189-232. On Jewish opposition to homosexuality see also Yarbrough, Not Like the Gentiles, 10, 19.

[18]Conzelmann, 1 Corinthians, 95-6. On the Greco-Roman view of incest see Foucault, The Care of the Self, 21-3. On Jewish opposition to incest see Yarbrough, Not Like the Gentiles, 9-10, 18-19. Yarbrough points out that Jews often regarded homosexuality and incest as behavior characteristic of Gentiles.

[19]See Philo's claim in Jos. 42-3 that although Gentiles patronize prostitutes, Jews do not do so at all. Musonius Rufus condemns sexual intercourse with a courtesan (hetaira - C. E. Lutz, Musonius Rufus "The Roman Socrates" [Yale Classical Studies 10; New Haven: Yale, 1947] 87). Dio Chrysostom attacks the existence of brothels (Or. 7.133-7; 77/78.4, 14).

[20]R. Scroggs has argued this in detail with respect to Paul's condemnation of homosexuality (The NT and Homosexuality, 99-122).

[21]Conzelmann, 1 Corinthians, 211. See also A. Wikenhauser, Die Kirche als der mystische Leib Christi nach dem Apostel Paulus (Münster: Aschendorff, 1937) 130-43.

[22]On this see A. Schweitzer, The Mysticism of Paul the Apostle trans. by W. Montgomery (New York: Holt, 1931): J. A. T. Robinson, The Body: A Study in Pauline Theology (SBT 5; London: SCM, 1952); E. Best, One Body in Christ: A Study of the Relationship of the Church to Christ in the Epistles of the Apostle Paul (London: SPCK, 1955).

[23]Cf. Hos 2:19-20; Jer 3:1; Ez 16:6-43; Is 54:5-6; 62:5. On these passages see Batey, NT Nuptial Imagery, 2-9.

[24]Plutarch also uses this last image, though without explicitly mentioning the mutual amalgamation of bodies, in Dialogue on Love 24 (Moralia 769 E-F). Cf. also Plutarch's comparison of marital union to grafting (Ibid.) and his comparison of the union of husband and wife to the union of soul and body (Advice to Bride and Groom 33; Moralia 142 E). On Plutarch's view of marriage see Foucault, The Care of the Self, 205-10.

[25]Translation of The Babylonian Talmud (London: Soncino, 1935-52). Similar interpretations of the verse are found in b. Sanh. 58b; p. Qidd. 1, 58c, 8 and Gen. Rab. 18.5.

[26]Meeks, "Image of the Androgyne," 185-9.

[27]On this see further T. Callan, "The Saying of Jesus in Gos. Thom. 22/2 Clem. 12/Gos. Eg. 5," forthcoming in JRS.

[28]Conzelman, 1 Corinthians, 114. On the rabbinic view of marriage as a duty see also Yarbrough, Not Like the Gentiles, 21-4.

[29]Foucault, The Use of Pleasure, 15-17, 20; The Care of the Self, 120-23; Rousselle, Porneia, 12-20 and elsewhere; Brown, The Body and Society, 19-20. Rousselle points out that Soranus and Galen attribute this view to Epicurus (Porneia, 12).

[30]Conzelmann, 1 Corinthians, 114-15. Conzelmann does not mention the views of the Epicureans. Yarbrough (Not Like the Gentiles, 32-41) discusses the divided opinion among Greco-Roman moralists concerning the value of marriage. Among critics of marriage he lists Epicurus, Diogenes the Cynic, and Theophrastus. On Epicurean and Cynic opposition to marriage see also Foucault, The Care of the Self, 154-9.
According to Diogenes Laertius, Diogenes the Cynic praised those who were about to marry and did not, those who were about to go on a voyage and did not, those who were about to engage in politics and did not, those who were about to raise children and did not, and those who were preparing to live with the powerful and never came near them (Lives 6.29; see also 54). That Diogenes' opposition to marriage did not imply sexual continence seems clear from stories about his public masturbation (Ibid. 6.46, 69). He may also have advocated sexual intercourse without marriage (Ibid.

6.72).

    D. L. Balch has shown that despite the generally
favorable attitude of the Stoics toward marriage,
Musonius Rufus, Epictetus and Hierocles all say that
marriage is not advantageous for some people. Further,
Epictetus and Hierocles both see avoidance of
distraction as one of the issues involved in deciding
whether or not to marry, as Paul does in 1 Cor 7:35 ("1
Cor 7:32-5 and Stoic Debates about Marriage, Anxiety
and Distraction," JBL 102 (1983) 429-39). In the case
of Epictetus, it is specifically the Cynic for whom
celibacy is desirable.

    [31]See Lucretius, de Rer. Nat. 4.1058-1287; cf. also
Epicurus, Vatican Fragments 51 and 80.

    [32]For the opposite view see Yarbrough, Not Like the
Gentiles, 105.

    [33]Meeks, "Image of the Androgyne," 178-9.

    [34]Similar views are found in b. Yebam. 63a-b; b.
Qidd. 29b and Yalkut Shim. on Deut 23:14.

    [35]Cf. Sir 9:1-9; T. Reuben 3.10-4.1; 5.1-7; 6.1-4;
T. Judah 15.5-6; 17; T. Issachar 4.4; b. Ber. 61a; b.
'Abod. Zar. 20a-b; b. Ned. 20a; m. 'Abot 1.5.

    [36]Meeks, "Image of the Androgyne," 177; Conzelmann,
1 Corinthians, 114; Yarbrough, Not Like the Gentiles,
60-62.

    [37]Conzelmann, 1 Corinthians, 116.

    [38]See Yarbrough, Not Like the Gentiles, 107-8.

    [39]Cf. T. Reuben 2.8-9; T. Issachar 2.3; T. Asher
5.1; Musonius Rufus, "On Sexual Indulgence" (Lutz,
Musonius Rufus, 87); Josephus, Ap. 2.199; Meeks, "Image
of the Androgyne," 177; Yarbrough, Not Like the
Gentiles, 11-12, 20-21.

    [40]On this see R. H. Gundry, "The Moral Frustration
of Paul Before His Conversion: Sexual Lust in Romans
7:7-25," Pauline Studies: Essays Presented to
Professor F. F. Bruce on his 70th Birthday ed. by D. A.
Hagner and M. J. Harris (Grand Rapids, MI: Eerdmans,
1980) 228-45; G. Theissen, Psychological Aspects of
Pauline Theology (Philadelphia: Fortress, 1987) 190-
201. Theissen argues that epithymia in Rom 7:7-8

includes sexual covetousness, but also refers to sin in general (pp 204-6).

[41]Others who have seen Paul's negative treatment of sexuality in 1 Corinthians 7, interpreted in light of Romans 7, as reflecting a personal difficulty with sexuality include O. Pfister, "Die Entwicklung des Apostels Paulus: Eine religionsgeschichtliche und psychologische Skizze," Imago 6 (1920) 243-90; Christianity and Fear: A Study in History and in the Psychology and Hygiene of Religion trans. by W. H. Johnson (London: Allen and Unwin, 1948) 223-4, 235. 266-7; S. Tarachow, "St. Paul and Early Christianity: A Psychoanalytic and Historical Study," Psychoanalysis and the Social Sciences 4 (1955) 232-3; and H. Fischer, Gespaltener christlicher Glaube: Eine psychoanalytisch orientierte Religionskritik (Hamburg: Reich, 1974) 52-6. Tarachow and Fischer apparently depend on Pfister, but go beyond him in suggesting that Paul was struggling against unconscious homosexual impulses. Tarachow seems to suggest this mainly on the basis of Paul's identification with Christ ("St. Paul and Early Christianity," 233, 236). Fischer argues chiefly on the basis of Paul's supposed special concern with homosexuality (Gespaltener christlicher Glaube, 54-6). Neither is very convincing to me.

G. Theissen has also argued that Paul favors repression of sexual impulses, though on very different grounds. Interpreting 2 Cor 3:4-4:6 and 1 Cor 11:3-16 together, and arguing that in both passages the veil serves as a symbol of the boundary between conscious and unconscious, Theissen concludes that while Paul is open to the superego's becoming conscious, he opposes the admission of the id into consciousness (Psychological Aspects of Pauline Theology, 115-75). Apart from questions about Theissen's exegesis of 1 Cor 11:3-16, one can ask whether it is possible to separate superego and id in this way. On this see the following discussion.

[42]For argument that the Oedipus complex was found among Greeks and Romans roughly contemporary with Paul, see T. W. Africa, "The Mask of an Assassin: A Psychohistorical Study of M. Junius Brutus," Journal of Interdisciplinary History 8 (1978) 599-626; "Psychohistory, Ancient History and Freud: The Descent into Avernus," Arethusa 12 (1979) 5-33. Africa relies largely, but not exclusively, on reports of Oedipal dreams. See also P. Gay, Freud for Historians (New

York/Oxford: Oxford University Press, 1985) 78-115,
especially pp. 93-9.

[43]C. Brenner, <u>An Elementary Textbook of Psycho-</u>
<u>analysis. Revised Edition</u> (Garden City, NY: Doubleday,
1974) 105-108.

[44]<u>Ibid</u>. 108.

[45]<u>Ibid</u>. 113.

[46]S. Freud, <u>Three Essays on the Theory of Sexuality</u>
reprinted in <u>The Standard Edition of the Complete</u>
<u>Psychological Works of Sigmund Freud</u> ed. by J. Strachey
(London: Hogarth, 1964) 7.178.

[47]Brenner, <u>An Elementary Textbook of Psycho-</u>
<u>analysis</u>, 117-18.

[48]<u>Ibid</u>. 118-19.

[49]S. Tarachow, "St. Paul and Early Christianity,"
232-3.

Chapter 4

Parent and Child

A. Paul's References to Parents and Children

Paul refers to his own parents only once (meter
Gal 1:15; but cf. Rom 16:13) and probably never refers
to his own childhood (but cf. 1 Cor 13:11).

However, Paul frequently speaks of parents and
children. Some of his references are to literal
parents and children. He mentions parents (goneis),[1]
mother (meter),[2] father (pater),[3] infants (nepioi Rom
2:20), sons (hyioi),[4] and children (tekna).[5] Many of
these references to parents and children are co-
ordinated with a reference to children and parents,
without making use of a noun meaning child or parent.[6]
He also refers to Rebecca's being pregnant (koiten
echousa Rom 9:10), to men in general as born through
women (1 Cor 11:12), to Jesus as born of woman (Gal
4:4) and to the begetting (gennao) of Ishmael and Isaac
(Gal 4:23, 29).

Another form of references to literal parents and
children consists of references to the relationship
between Jesus, Paul, or other Jews and their more
distant ancestors. He speaks of Jesus as seed (sperma)
of David (Rom 1:3; cf. 2 Tim 2:8), and seed of Abraham
(Gal 3:16, 19), and of himself (Rom 11:1; 2 Cor 11:22)
and others (2 Cor 11:22) as seed of Abraham. He also
quotes Is 1:9 which refers to the seed of the people of
Israel (Rom 9:29). Paul mentions children (tekna) of
Abraham (Rom 9:7, 8) and sons (hyioi) of Israel (Rom

9:27; 2 Cor 3:7, 13). And once he refers to descendants of Israel without using a noun (Rom 9:6). Correspondingly Paul speaks of Abraham as forefather (propater Rom 4:1), Isaac as father (pater Rom 9:10), and refers simply to the fathers (patres)[7] and the paternal (patrikon) traditions (Gal 1:14).[8]

Even more often than he speaks of literal parents and children, Paul uses language about parents and children figuratively. Once he makes use of the Semitic idiom according to which 'son of' indicates relationship in general: sons of light and sons of day (hyioi 1 Thess 5:5).[9] Once he also makes use of the corresponding Semitic idiom 'father of,' describing God as father of mercies (pater 2 Cor 1:3).

Another sort of figurative use of language about parents and children can be seen in Paul's understanding of Abraham as the father of those who believe in Jesus. Abraham is called father (pater)[10] and believers are called his seed (sperma),[11] children (tekna Rom 9:7-8), or sons (hyioi Gal 3:7). This understanding is worked out most fully in Paul's allegorical interpretation of the children of Abraham and their mothers in Gal 4:22-31: Hagar stands for the Sinai covenant bearing children (gennosa) into slavery (v 24); she also corresponds to the present Jerusalem who serves with her children (teknon v 25); Jerusalem above is our mother (meter v 26); you are children according to the promise (tekna v 28); we are not children (tekna) of the slave but of the free woman (v 31).

In 1 Cor 14:20 Paul uses childhood as a metaphor for inexperience and urges his readers not to be

children (paidia) with respect to thought, but to be
children (nepiazete) with respect to evil. According
to some manuscripts, in 1 Thess 2:7 Paul uses childhood
as a metaphor for gentleness and says that he was a
child (nepios) when he was with the Thessalonians.

Paul uses childbirth as an image of suddenness
(odin 1 Thess 5:3) and pain (1 Thess 5:3; synodino Rom
8:22; odino Gal 4:19). He also uses it as an image of
incompletion (Rom 8:22; Gal 4:19, 27). In 1 Cor 15:8
Paul uses the incompletion of the aborted or miscarried
fetus (ektroma) as an image, probably expressing his
'monstrous' character as a persecutor of the church.
Paul also uses childhood itself as an image of
incompletion. He describes the Corinthians as babes
(nepioi) in Christ who need milk, not solid food (1 Cor
3:1-2). In two other places he uses the figure of the
child (nepios) as an image of an imperfect state (1 Cor
13:11; Gal 4:1, 3; cf. Eph 4:14-15). He presents
childhood as an imperfect state in another way by
speaking of it as subjection to the pedagogue
(paidagogos Gal 3:24-5) and the father (pater Gal 4:2).

Rather commonly Paul uses the language of parent
and child as a metaphor for his relationship with
others. He can use it to speak of his relationship
with individuals. He speaks of Rufus's mother (meter)
and mine (Rom 16:13), calls Timothy his child
(teknon),[12] and likewise calls Onesimus his child (Phm
10). Paul explicitly calls himself Timothy's father
(pater Phil 2:22) and says that he has begotten
Onesimus (egennesa Phm 10).

Paul can also use this language to speak of his
relationship with his churches. He speaks of his

churches as children (tekna)[13] and himself as their
father (pater),[14] parent (goneus 2 Cor 12:14) or nurse
(trophos 1 Thess 2:7). Paul also says that he begot
(egennesa) the Corinthians in Christ (1 Cor 4:15) and
that he is again in travail with the Galatians (Gal
4:19). Further he says that he fed the Corinthians
with milk (like a mother or a nurse?) (1 Cor 3:1-2) and
that he betrothed them to Christ (acting as a father?)
(2 Cor 11:2).[15]

Most commonly of all Paul uses the language of
parent and child as a metaphor for the relationship of
God to others. At times Paul simply calls God father
(pater).[16] More often he specifies that God is the
father of Jesus.[17] He refers to Jesus as his son
(hyios) where God is the antecedent of 'his.'[18] Paul
also refers to Jesus as son (hyios) of God.[19] Once
Paul simply refers to Jesus as the son (hyios 1 Cor
15:28).

Paul also frequently specifies that God is the
father of his people. He frequently refers to God as
our father (pater),[20] or our God and father.[21] Twice
Paul says that Christians can call God 'Abba, Father'
(pater Rom 8:15; Gal 4:6). In 2 Cor 6:18 Paul quotes
God as saying 'I will be your father (pater).[22] Paul
speaks of the sons (hyioi) of God,[23] the children
(tekna) of God,[24] the seed (sperma) of God (Rom 9:8),
and daughters (thygaterai) of God (2 Cor 6:18). He
also speaks of sonship (hyothesia) of God.[25] Once Paul
refers to Jesus as the firstborn of many brothers
(adelphoi Rom 8:29).

Paul's literal use of language about parents and
children appears to be fairly neutral. His figurative

use of this language, especially to describe his and God's relationships with others, is very positive; for Paul the relationship of parents to children is an image of intimacy and love. It seems likely that this reflects Paul's conscious attitude toward the parent-child relationship in general, and toward his own relationship with his parents in particular. It is especially striking that Paul several times uses this language to compare himself to a mother (Gal 4:19; 1 Cor 3:1-2) or a nurse (1 Thess 2:7).

On the other hand, some of Paul's figurative use of this language, especially to describe difficulty or incompletion, is rather negative. This may imply a negative attitude in Paul toward parents and being a parent, and even more toward children and being a child. Perhaps Paul also had negative feelings about his own childhood and his relationship with his parents. If so, these are likely to have been less conscious than his positive feelings. This seems to follow first of all from the preponderance of positive references to parents and children. But it is also strongly suggested by Paul's failure to discuss the Akedah.

In Paul's extensive discussion of Abraham in Romans 4 and Galatians 3, he never mentions the single most striking episode in the life of Abraham, namely, the binding of Isaac. This in itself is suggestive. But when it is combined with the observation that Paul does refer to the Akedah obliquely in Rom 8:32, it seems very likely that Paul is repressing this element of the story of Abraham. In Rom 8:32 Paul says that God did not spare his own son, but gave him over on behalf of us all. This seems to pick up the language of Gen 22:16 which describes Abraham's willingness not to spare his son. N. A. Dahl has argued that in this verse Paul understands the crucifixion of Jesus as an adequate reward for the Akedah, i.e., as an appropriate return on God's part for Abraham's faith in being willing to sacrifice Isaac.[26]

Thus Paul can make use of this story though only in the form of a brief allusion which would escape casual notice. This makes it seem very likely that the omission of this story from Paul's extensive discussion of Abraham is no accident, but rather the result of repression. And it seems quite plausible that Paul represses this because it presents the relationship of father to son negatively, which is something Paul does not wish to confront. And this in turn may be because Paul has negative feelings about his own father's relationship with him, which he cannot recognize.[27]

B. The Cultural Context of Paul's References to Parents and Children

Paul's literal use of the language of parent and child seems to require no further discussion. The same is true of his figurative use of this language, when it is neutral. What is necessary is to locate Paul's positive and negative uses of this imagery in his cultural context in order to see their significance more clearly.

Paul's use of the relationship between parent and child as a metaphor for his relationship to others has abundant parallels in his cultural milieu. P. Gutierrez has studied "The Metaphor of Paternity in

Antiquity."[28]   He mentions that Deborah is called
mother ('m; meter) of Israel in Judges 5:7 and shows
that various persons are called 'father' ('b; pater) in
a figurative sense in the Bible: the counselor of the
king (e.g., Gen 45:8; Is 22:21), the priest (e.g.,
Judges 17:10; 18:19), the prophet (e.g., 2 Kings 2:12;
6:21; 13:14), the teacher of wisdom (e.g., Prov 4:1).
The recipients of wisdom teaching are also frequently
called son (bn; hyios e.g., Prov 1:8, 10, 15), child
(teknon e.g. Sir 2:1) or children (bnym; paides e.g.,
Prov 4:1; tekna Sir 3:1).   In addition to these
biblical uses of the metaphor, Gutierrez also finds it
in   the   Qumran   literature: the   recipients   of
instruction are addressed as sons (bnym) in CD 2.14;
the guardian of the camp is compared to a father ('ab)
with his children (bnym) in CD 13.9, as is the speaker
in 1 QH 7.20-22.   He also finds it in Philo.   For
example, Philo says that we think of the standard-
bearers of noble living as fathers who begot us
(gennetas kai pateras Conf. 149).   Roman authorities
were given the title 'father,' as when Cicero was
called father (pater) of his country.[29] Gutierrez also
finds the metaphor used in connection with mystery
religions.   For example, in Apuleius' Metamorphoses
11.21.3 and 25.7 Lucius compares the priest who
presided over his initiation into the mysteries of Isis
to a parent (parens).   Finally, Gutierrez also finds
the   metaphor   used   in   Hellenistic   religious
associations, the Hermetic literature, magic and the
rabbinic literature.   The most striking use of the
metaphor in rabbinic literature is the statement found
in b. Sanh. 19b: If anyone instructs the son of

another in the law, it is as if he had begotten him
(yldw).

In summary Gutierrez says that the metaphor of
paternity has been used most often to describe the
activity of the priest and that of the teacher, with
the   latter   being   by   far   the   more   frequent
application.[30]

In addition to the examples of the use of this
metaphor discussed by Gutierrez, we also find it in
Philo, Leg. 58 where Macro says that he has begotten
(gegenneka) Gaius more than have his parents (goneon).
Pliny compares the commonwealth to a daughter (filia
Epist. 4.13) and quaestors (4.15) and himself (6.12) to
sons (filii). He also compares the commonwealth to a
parent (parens 4.13) and himself to a father (pater
5.19).   And according to Suetonius, Julius Caesar
called Brutus 'child' (teknon).

Paul's use of the relationship between mother and
child to describe his relationship to his churches also
has parallels, but in this Paul seems more distinctive.
We may first of all consider 1 Thess 2:7 where Paul
compares himself to a nurse (trophos), perhaps meaning
a mother. According to Gutierrez we find a similar use
of this image in Num 11:12 where Moses says that God
tells him to carry the people in his arms like a nurse
('mn; cf. Is 49:23). Similarly in 1 QH 7.20-22 the
speaker says that God has made him a nurse to the men
of marvel.[31] A. J. Malherbe has shown that Paul's use
of the image of the nurse in 1 Thess 2:7 corresponds to
widespread use of this image by Cynic philosophers.[32]
Thus Paul's use of maternal imagery in 1 Thess 2:7
seems fairly conventional.

A second passage in which Paul uses maternal imagery to describe his relationship with one of his churches is 1 Cor 3:1-2.   Here he says that the Corinthians were babes (nepioi) in Christ and so he gave them milk to drink and not solid food. The use of infancy as an image for an early stage of development, and even the use of milk as an image for the instruction which is appropriate to that stage, is common in Paul's cultural milieu. We find the former in Philo, Sobr. 9, the latter in Epictetus 3.24.9, and both in various passages.[33]   Although Paul is making use of conventional imagery here, he uses it more personally than Philo or Epictetus.   For example, in Agr. 9 Philo says that for babes (nepioi) milk (gala) is food, but for grown men, wheaten bread.   In content this is very close to what Paul says in 1 Cor 3:1-2. But Philo's use of the image is impersonal and objective; it leaves him uninvolved in the feeding. By contrast Paul says that he gave the Corinthians milk to drink, using the image in a way that casts him in the role of mother or nurse.   There do not seem to be any parallels to this.

A third passage in which Paul uses maternal imagery is Gal 4:19 where he addresses the Galatians as his children with whom he is again in labor. The use of motherhood as an image for the relationship between people is not unprecedented.[34]   In the Bible we find it used to describe the relationship of God to God's people (Is 49:15; 66:13; cf. Sir 4:10).[35] We find this same usage in 1 QH 9.35-6 where God's love for the men of truth is compared to that of a woman who loves her child, or that of a nurse.   According to H. D. Betz, comparison with a loving mother was part of the friendship theme; he cites texts from Plato, Aristotle, Plutarch and Cicero. But Betz says that the idea of Paul's giving birth to the Galatians has parallels only in gnosticism and he cites Disc. 8-9: "The son asks (53.15ff): 'my father, do they also have mothers?' Whereupon Hermes Trismegistus answers: 'my son, they are spiritual [mothers]. For they are potencies; they let the souls grow. Therefore I say, they are immortal.'"[36]

The translation of this passage is uncertain. But even if the translation used by Betz is correct, it is not at all clear who are the 'mothers' being referred to; and the description of their motherhood is not very close to Paul's language in Gal 4:19. Much closer is the description of God as the mother who gave birth to Israel in Deut 32:18 and Is 45:10 (cf. also Is 42:14). However, in Is 45:10 and probably in Deut 32:18, God is compared both to father and mother, while in Is 42:13-14 God is compared to a warrior and a mother; this has the effect of de-emphasizing the comparison with either. By contrast Paul compares himself only to a mother in Gal 4:19. In addition Paul pictures himself as being in the midst of the labor contractions which will bring the Galatians to birth. The only parallel to this is Is 42:14, but in this passage the image is used less personally and realistically than in Gal 4:19.

Thus Paul's use of maternal imagery in 1 Cor 3:1-2 and Gal 4:19 seems to go beyond what we find elsewhere in his cultural context. This makes it seem possible that his use of this imagery is particularly reflective of Paul's personality.

Turning to Paul's use of the language of parent and child to describe the relationship of God to others, we once again find abundant parallels.[37]   In the Bible the people of Israel are called son (bn; hyios) of God[38] or first-born (bkr; prototokos) of God (Exod 4:22; Jer 31:8 [LXX 38:9]; cf. Sir 36:11 protogonos). Likewise God is called father ('b; pater) of Israel.[39] In Mal 1:6 God is compared to a father and the priests to his sons (bn; hyios). God is also said to be father of the king and the king his son.[40] The portrayal of God as father becomes even more common in post-biblical Judaism. We find it in 1 QH 9.35 where God is addressed as father ('b) of the sons (bnym) of his truth. Philo calls God father (pater) of all (e.g., Fug. 109; Conf. 63; Spec. Leg. 2.6) or of the world (e.g., Spec. Leg. 1.96), the father of the Logos (e.g., Conf. 63; cf. 146) and the father of Moses (Q Exod. 2.46). Josephus likewise calls God the father of all.[41] And God is frequently seen as father in rabbinic literature. For example, in m. 'Abot 3.14 R. Akiba is quoted as saying: Beloved are the Israelites in that they are called sons of God; still more beloved in that it is made known to them that they are sons of God (in Deut 14:1). The expression 'father in heaven' is especially common.[42]

The portrayal of God as father is also common in Greek and Roman writers. In Homer Zeus is called father (pater) of men and gods. Plato refers to the maker of the universe as its father (Timaeus 28 C; 37 C). Musonius Rufus refers to Zeus as father.[43] Epictetus also calls God father (1.3.1; 3.24.3).

What naturally lacks any parallel in non-Christian sources is the presentation of Jesus as son of God. However, this seems so widespread in early Christianity that it need have no significance for Paul beyond that which it has for other Christians.

Paul's use of childbirth as a metaphor for suddenness (1 Thess 5:3) does not have many parallels. However, his use of childbirth as a metaphor for pain (1 Thess 5:3; Rom 8:22; Gal 4:19) has abundant parallels, especially in the Bible.[44] There we find many references to anguish like a woman's in labor.[45] In Is 66:7-9 we find miraculous escape from the pains of childbirth used as an image. We also have references to childbirth as a metaphor for pain in the Qumran literature: 1 QH 3.7-12; 5.30-32.[46] And we find it in 1 Enoch 62.4 and 4 Ezra 4.42.

Similarly Paul's use of childbirth as a metaphor for incompletion (Rom 8:22; Gal 4:19) has parallels in the Bible (Is 26:16-18; 37:3 [= 2 Kings 19:3]; 66:7-9) and the Qumran literature (1 QH 3.7-12). Related to this is the idea of the labor pains of the messianic age.[47]

All of this makes it seem likely that in using childbirth as a metaphor for pain and incompletion, the Qumran literature and Paul are both making use of biblical imagery.

Paul's use of the aborted or miscarried fetus as an image of monstrous imperfection has parallels in the Bible and in Philo. Ektroma is used as an image to describe leprosy in Num 12:12, and as the term of comparison for an unfortunate person in Job 31:16; Eccl 6:3. Philo uses the word to describe the offspring of

the unworthy person's soul (L. A. 1.76). Thus Paul
seems to be using a conventional image, but he applies
it to himself. This may indicate that it has
particular meaning for him.[48] This might still be true
even if Paul is only adapting a word used by his
critics.

Paul's use of childhood as a metaphor for
incompletion also has parallels.[49] The contrast
between milk and solid food in 1 Cor 3:1-2 has
parallels as we have seen above.[50] Likewise the
broader contrast between the child and the adult in 1
Cor 13:11 also has parallels. Compare Epictetus, Ench.
5.1: You are no longer a lad (meirakion) but already a
full grown man; and Seneca, Ep. Mor. 4.2: You laid
aside the garment of boyhood (praetexta) and donned
man's toga; 27.2: Count your years and you will be
ashamed to pursue the same things you desired in your
boyhood days (puer). Once again, however, Paul applies
this conventional image to himself, perhaps indicating
that it has particular meaning for him.

Paul's use of the situation of one under a
pedagogue as an image for those under the law in Gal
3:24-5 makes use of a well-known figure of antiquity.[51]
The pedagogue was the slave who accompanied the child
to school and back, carried the child's books and
writing implements, protected the child from harm, and
taught the child good manners. The pedagogue was used
as an image with a positive value, as when Philo
compares the pedagogue who keeps the child from going
astray, to the watchful eye of God (Mut. 217). Paul
may be using the image this way in 1 Cor 4:15. On the
other hand the image of the pedagogue was used

negatively, as when Plutarch contrasts giving advice in the manner of a friend with giving it in the manner of a pedagogue (paidagogikos), i.e., in the form of a stream of petty accusations (Moralia 73 A). In Gal 3:24-5 Paul uses the image in this latter sense.

And finally, Paul's use of the image of the child in Gal 4:1-3 draws upon Roman law. According to H. D. Betz, Paul is referring to the Roman legal practice of guardianship for a minor, specifically one established by testament. This was an arrangement by which a father appointed one or more guardians for his children during a period of time before they would be able to dispose of their inheritance. As Betz notes, the equation of the minor in such a situation with a slave is hyperbolic; the two are similar in lacking the capacity for self determination, but are also vastly different.[52] Possibly Paul's equation of the minor with the slave betrays a negative attitude on his part toward childhood.

All of this suggests that Paul's use of childhood as an image of incompletion, while derived from his culture, may be unusually negative and in that way betray his own bias.

The history of the interpretation of the binding of Isaac (Genesis 22) has been written by S. Spiegel.[53] The Akedah is included in most accounts of Abraham which are roughly contemporary with Paul.[54] The only contemporary parallel to Paul's omission of the Akedah from his account of Abraham is the similar omission from the account of Abraham in the Biblical Antiquities of Pseudo-Philo (see Bib. Ant. 8). However, unlike Paul, Pseudo-Philo mentions the Akedah at three other

points (18.5; 32.2-4; 40.2), and the second of these is
a fairly extensive discussion. Thus it is clear that
Paul's oblique reference to the story of the Akedah is
striking in his cultural context and may betray its
sensitivity for him.

C. Psychological Analysis of Paul's References to Parents and Children

We noted above that Paul's literal references to
parents and children, and some of his figurative use of
this language, are fairly neutral. We also noted that
most of his figurative use of this language is very
positive. When he uses it to describe his and God's
relationships to others, it serves to characterize
these relationships as intimate and loving. I further
suggested that this may be Paul's most conscious
attitude toward the parent-child relationship and
toward his own relationship with his parents. We have
now seen that the figurative use of the language of
parent and child to characterize the relationships of
God and others to someone else, is widespread in Paul's
cultural milieu and may be described as conventional.
However, it still seems likely that this indicates
Paul's most conscious attitude toward parents and
children, including his own relationship with his
parents; we must simply note that this is an attitude
which Paul shares with his culture.

Alongside the positive use of figurative language
about parents and children, we also find a negative use
of this language in Paul. He uses childbirth as an
image of pain and incompletion and childhood itself as
an image of incompletion. I suggested above that this

represents a less conscious view of parents and children, and of Paul's own relationship with his parents. We have now seen that the figurative use of language about parents and children in this negative sense is also widespread in Paul's cultural milieu. Once again this seems to mean that Paul shares this attitude with his culture; both Paul and his culture have ambivalent attitudes toward parents and children. In Paul's case at least, the positive attitude dominates.

It seems noteworthy that the ambivalence Paul shares with his culture with respect to parents differs according to the sex of the parent. On the positive side, the relationship of both father and mother to the child is seen as intimate and loving. But the negative aspect of the father is the threat he poses to the child, while the negative aspect of the mother is what might be called the threat which the child poses to her, i.e., the suffering she undergoes in being a mother. Thus in the case of fathers, it is their attitude toward their children which is seen as ambivalent, while in the case of the mother it is mainly the state of motherhood itself which is seen as ambivalent, i.e., as something which involves suffering for the mother as well as a positive relationship with the child. Of course, the suffering of the mother can easily result in a negative attitude toward the child, and likewise the negative attitude of the father rests on a threat posed by the child. Only the first of these is at all explicit in Paul (cf. 1 Cor 3:1-2; Gal 4:19).

Some elements of Paul's negative use of language about parents and children are peculiar to him. This is true above all of his treatment of the Akedah. As we have noted, Paul omits any reference to this from his lengthy discussion of Abraham in Romans 4 and Galatians 3, but then alludes to it in Rom 8:32. We have also seen that in doing this Paul differs from his contemporaries, who discuss the Akedah fully in treating Abraham. This makes it highly likely that Paul is repressing the story of the Akedah, with its presentation of a father who nearly sacrifices his son. And it seems quite likely that Paul represses this in order to avoid confronting negative feelings about his own relationship with his father. And at the same time Paul may well be repressing negative feelings about his relationship with God as father.

The existence of an unconscious, negative attitude toward fathers, and especially his father, is confirmed by Paul's statement that the minor, while under his father's provision of guardianship, is no better than a slave (Gal 4:1). As we have noted, this is an exaggeration and may reveal Paul's own negative feelings about being a child in relationship to his father.

In terms of Freudian psychology we can account for this by reference to Paul's resolution of the Oedipus complex. Paul abandoned his incestuous desire for his mother out of fear of his father, particularly fear of castration. He did so primarily by identifying with his father, thus repressing his fear of his father. This would account both for his predominantly positive attitude toward fathers and also for the traces of a negative attitude toward fathers in Paul. E. Wellisch has shown how easily the Akedah can be understood in terms of the Oedipal drama.[55]

It is tempting to speculate that Paul's negative attitude toward fathers, and his father, and toward being a child, may also have resulted from his having been in the situation he describes in Gal 4:1-3. Having been in this situation would account in another way for the excessively negative assessment of it which we have noted.

In addition to the elements of Paul's negative use of language about parents and children which are peculiar to him, there are also elements of Paul's positive use of this language which are peculiar to him. As we have seen, these elements are Paul's uses of maternal imagery to describe his relationship to his churches; these go beyond anything to be found in Paul's culture.

This too can be accounted for by appeal to Paul's resolution of the Oedipus complex. He may have abandoned his incestuous desire for his mother not only by identifying with his father, but also by identifying with his mother. This would produce a homosexual element in Paul's personality, which balances the heterosexual identification with his father. In the terms of Jungian psychology, we might speak of a balance between animus and anima in Paul.[56]

Of course, psychoanalytic theory postulates the universality of the Oedipus complex. If it is universal, then this resolution of the Oedipus complex would be common and might underlie the ambivalence about parents and children which Paul shares with his culture. We can account for the manifestations of a negative attitude toward fathers and a positive attitude toward mothers which are peculiar to Paul by postulating either an unusually strong desire for his mother in Paul, or an unusually strong prohibition of this desire on the part of his parents, or both.

When Paul finally does refer to the Akedah, it is an allusion which directly refers to God's sacrifice of his son, Jesus. Perhaps as a result of his conversion, Paul was able to acknowledge consciously the negative aspect of God as father and of his natural father. This may have occurred because Paul understands being a Christian as union with Jesus in his death and resurrection, and thus sees death at the hands of the father as finally not threatening.

Notes

[1]Rom 1:30; cf. Eph 6:1; Col 3:20; 2 Tim 3:2; progoneis in 1 Tim 5:4.

[2]Rom 16:13; cf. Eph 5:31; 6:2; 2 Tim 1:5.

[3]1 Cor 5:1; cf. Eph 5:31; 6:2, 4; Col 3:21.

[4]Rom 9:9; Gal 4:22, 30 (three times).

[5]1 Cor 7:14; cf. Eph 6:1; Col 3:20; Eph 6:4; Col 3:21; 1 Tim 3:4; Titus 1:6; 1 Tim 3:12; 5:4; cf. also teknogonias (1 Tim 2:15), eteknotrophesen (1 Tim 5:10), teknogonein (1 Tim 5:14), and philoteknous (Titus 2:4); cf. also brephos (2 Tim 3:15).

[6]Rom 1:30; 9:9; 16:13; 1 Cor 5:1; 7:14; Gal 4:22, 30; cf. Eph 5:31; 1 Tim 3:4; Titus 1:6; 1 Tim 3:12; 5:4; 2 Tim 1:5; 3:2.

[7]Rom 9:5; 11:28; 15:8; 1 Cor 10:1.

[8]Cf. references to fathers (progonon) of Paul (2 Tim 1:3) and to Timothy's grandmother (mamme 2 Tim 1:5).

[9]Cf. sons (hyioi) of disobedience (Eph 2:2; 5:6; Col 3:6), sons of men (Eph 3:5), son of perdition (2 Thess 2:3); cf. also children (tekna) of wrath (Eph 2:3), children of light (Eph 5:8).

[10]Rom 4:11, 12 (twice), 16, 17, 18.

[11]Rom 4:13, 16, 18; Gal 3:29.

[12]1 Cor 4:17; Phil 2:22; cf. 1 Tim 1:2, 18; 2 Tim 1:2; 2:1; cf. also Titus as Paul's child (Titus 1:4).

[13]1 Cor 4:14; 2 Cor 6:13; 12:14; Gal 4:19; 1 Thess 2:7, 11.

[14]1 Cor 4:15, here contrasting himself with their pedagogues (paidagogoi); 1 Thess 2:11.

[15]Cf. also the exhortation to Timothy to treat older men as fathers and older women as mothers in 1 Tim 5:1-2.

[16]Rom 6:4; 1 Cor 8:6; 15:24; Gal 1:1, 3; Phil 2:11; 1 Thess 1:1; cf. Eph 1:17; 2:18; 3:14-15; 5:20; 6:23; Col 1:12; 3:17; 2 Thess 1:2; 1 Tim 1:1; 2 Tim 1:2; Titus 1:4.

[17]Rom 15:6; 2 Cor 1:3; 11:31; cf. Eph 1:3; Col 1:3.

[18]Rom 1:3, 9; 5:10; 8:3, 29, 32; 1 Cor 1:9; Gal 1:16; 4:4, 6; 1 Thess 1:10; cf. Col 1:13.

[19]Rom 1:4; 2 Cor 1:19; Gal 2:20; cf. Eph 4:13.

[20]Rom 1:7; 1 Cor 1:3; 2 Cor 1:2; Phil 1:2; 1 Thess 3:11; Phm 3; cf. Eph 1:2; Col 1:2; 2 Thess 1:1; 2:16.

[21]Gal 1:4; Phil 4:20; 1 Thess 1:3; 3:13.

[22]Cf. God as father (pater) of all in Eph 4:6.

[23]Rom 8:14, 19; 9:26; 2 Cor 6:18; Gal 3:26; 4:6, 7.

[24]Rom 8:16, 17, 21; 9:8; Phil 2:15; cf. Eph 5:1.

[25]Rom 8:15, 23; 9:4; Gal 4:5; cf. Eph 1:5.

[26]N. A. Dahl, "The Atonement - An Adequate Reward for the Akedah?" The Crucified Messiah and Other Essays (Minneapolis: Augsburg, 1974) 146-60; cf. also H. J. Schoeps, Paul: The Theology of the Apostle in the Light of Jewish Religious History trans. by H. Knight (Philadelphia: Westminster, 1961) 141-9.

[27]G. Theissen (Psychological Aspects of Pauline Theology trans. by J. P. Galvin [Philadelphia: Fortress, 1987] 47) mentions Paul's treatment of the Akedah as an example of the omission of a certain theme where it might be expected and its appearance in a different context (see p 8 above). Theissen also thinks that the omission reveals Paul's unconscious, but he interprets the omission in a different way.

[28]Pedro Gutierrez, La Paternité Spirituelle selon Saint Paul (Études Bibliques; Paris: Gabalda, 1968) 15-83; cf. also G. Schrenk, G. Quell, "pater ktl.," TDNT 5.945-1022; W. Grundmann, "Die NEPIOI in der urchristlichen Paränese," NTS 5 (1958-9) 188-205; P. A. H. De Boer, Fatherhood and Motherhood in Israelite and Judean Piety (Leiden: Brill, 1974) especially pp 14-25; E. Best, Paul and His Converts: The Sprunt Lectures 1985 (Edinburgh: T. & T. Clark, 1988) 34-5.

[29]On this see also J. H. Elliott, A Home for the Homeless: A Sociological Exegesis of 1 Peter, Its Situation and Strategy (Philadelphia: Fortress, 1981) 175-9.

[30]Gutierrez, Paternité, 82.

[31]Ibid., 97-9.

[32]A. J. Malherbe, "'Gentle as a Nurse:' The Cynic Background to 1 Thess 2," NovT 12 (1970) 203-17.

[33]Philo, Agr. 9; Migr. 29; Congr. 19; Somn. 2.10; Probus 160; and Epictetus 2.16.39. Cf. also Heb 5:12-14.

[34]Motherhood is also frequently used as an image for other things. In Ps 7:15; Job 15:35; Is 59:4 it is used to describe what a person has accomplished. Philo uses motherhood as an image to describe nature as productive (Probus 79) and likewise the soul (L. A. 3.150; Congr. 66; 129) and knowledge (Eb. 30-33) as productive. On Philo see also G. Bertram, "odin ktl.," TDNT 9.671.

[35]On these and other passages which present God as mother see M. I. Gruber, "The Motherhood of God in Second Isaiah," RB 90 (1983) 351-9; P. Trible, God and the Rhetoric of Sexuality (Overtures to Biblical Theology; Philadelphia: Fortress, 1978) 31-71; L. Swidler, Biblical Affirmations of Women (Philadelphia: Westminster, 1979) 30-36.

[36]H. D. Betz, Galatians (Hermeneia; Philadelphia: Fortress, 1979) 233-4, quoting the translation of Karl-Wolfgang Troeger et. al., "Die sechste und siebte Schrift aus Nag Hammadi-Codex VI," TLZ 98 (1973) 495-503, 498f.

[37]See discussions of this in G. F. Moore, Judaism in the First Centuries of the Christian Era, the Age of the Tannaim (New York: Schocken, 1971) [original publication 1927, 1930] 2.201-11; G. Schrenk, G. Quell, "pater ktl.," 951-9, 965-74, 978-82; M. Hengel, The Son of God: The Origin of Christology and the History of Jewish-Hellenistic Religion (Philadelphia: Fortress, 1976) 21-56.

[38]Exod 4:22; Deut 14:1; Jer 3:19 (tekna); 31:19 [LXX 38:20]; Hos 11:1 (nepios); cf. Wis 18:4.

[39]Deut 32:6; Is 45:10; 63:16; Jer 3:4, 19; 31:8 [LXX 38:9]; Mal 2:10.

[40]2 Sam 7:14; Pss 2:7; 89:27-8 [LXX 88:27-8]. Pss 2:7 and 110:3 [LXX 109:3] speak of God's begetting (yld; gennao) the king.

[41]E.g., Ant. 1.20, 230; 2.152; 7.380.

[42]Moore, Judaism, 2.204-9.

[43]C. E. Lutz, Musonius Rufus "The Roman Socrates" (Yale Classical Studies 10; New Haven: Yale, 1947) 65, 107.

[44]On this topic see G. Bertram, "odin," 667-74.

[45]hyl kywldh = odines hos tiktouses (Ps 48:7 [LXX 47:7]; Jer 6:24; 50:43 [LXX 27:43]; Micah 4:9); syrym whblym...kywldh = odines...hos gynaikos tiktouses (Is 13:8); ksyry ywldh = odines...hos ten tiktousan (Is 21:3); kmw hrh tqryb lldt thyl = hos he odinousa eggizei tou tekein (Is 26:17); khwlh...srh kmbkyrh = hos odinouses...tou stenagmou sou hos prototokouses

(Jer 4:31);   hblym...kmw 'st ldh = odines...kathos
gynaika tiktousan (Jer 13:21); hblym hyl kyldh = odinas
hos tiktouses (Jer 22:23); hlsyw kywlydh (Jer 30:6 [LXX
omits]); klb 'sh msrh = hos kardia gynaikos odinouses
(Jer 48:41 [LXX omits]; 49:22 [LXX 30:16]); srh
whblym...kywldh (Jer 49:24 [LXX omits]).

[46]kmw 'st ldh mbkryh (1 QH 3.7); ksvry ywldh (1 QH
5.30-31). Cf. also John 16:21; Ignatius, Rom. 6.1.

[47]On this see Moore, Judaism 2.361; G. Bertram,
"odin," 672-3. Cf. also Matt 24:8; Rev 12:2-3.

[48]Ignatius, perhaps in dependence on 1 Cor 15:8-10,
also uses the image for himself in Rom. 9.2.

[49]On this topic see G. Bertram, "nepios ktl.," TDNT
4.912-23.

[50]Cf. Ignatius, Trall. 5.1.

[51]On this see Betz, Galatians, 177-80; D. J. Lull,
"'The Law Was Our Pedagogue:'   A Study in Galatians
3:19-25," JBL 105 (1986) 489-95.

[52]Betz, Galatians, 202-4.

[53]S. Spiegel, The Last Trial, trans. by J. Goldin
(New York: Schocken, 1967); cf. also G. Vermes,
"Redemption and Genesis XXII," Scripture and Tradition
(Leiden: Brill, 1961) 193-227.

[54]See for example Jub. 18; Philo, Abr. 167-199;
James 2:21-3; Heb 11:17-19; Josephus, Ant. 1.223-36;
Gen. Rab. 55-6.

[55]E. Wellisch, "The Oedipus Conflict in the
Akedah," Isaac and Oedipus (London: Routledge and
Kegan Paul, 1954) 74-97.   See also D. F. Zeligs,
Psychoanalysis and the Bible: A Study in Depth of
Seven Leaders (New York: Human Sciences Press, 1988)
31-3.

[56]On this see M. A. Mattoon, Jungian Psychology in
Perspective (New York: Free Press, 1981) 95-101.

Chapter 5

Death

A. Paul's View of Death

Despite some neutral references to death as simply a part of human experience,[1] it is clear that Paul's basic attitude toward death is negative.[2] This is obvious from references to killing as something bad[3] and to death as an extreme misfortune.[4] A negative view is strongly implied in references to resurrection from the dead which suggest that death is something to be escaped[5] and in the use of death as an image for some undesirable state.[6]

Above all Paul's negative view of death is clear from the connection which Paul sees between sin and death.[7] This connection is explicated at greatest length in Rom 5:12-21 (cf. 1 Cor 15:21-2). Death came into the world through the sin of one man (v 12, 15) and spread to all because all sinned (v 12). Since the time of Adam death has reigned (v 14, 17), or rather sin has reigned through death (v 21), in that all die as a result of sin.[8]

Paul uses various images to describe the relationship between sin and death: death is the wage of sin (Rom 6:21-3), death is the fruit of sin (Rom 7:5), sin works death (Rom 7:13), sin is the sting of death (1 Cor 15:56). But the basic idea seems to be that death is a punishment for sin (cf. 1 Cor 11:30), specifically a legal punishment (cf. Rom 1:32). This means that the law is intimately involved in the

relationship between sin and death.[9]   Sin is first
reckoned after the law was given (Rom 5:13). The law
was given to increase sin (Rom 5:20; cf. Gal 3:19). It
did so not only by making sin known as sin, but also by
arousing sin in human beings (Rom 7:5), by setting an
ideal before them without providing any power to attain
it (Rom 7:7-20; cf. Gal 3:10-13). Thus Paul can speak
of the law of sin and death (Rom 8:2) and equate being
dominated by sin with being under the law (Rom 6:14).
In 1 Cor 15:56 he says that the law is the power of
sin; in 2 Cor 3:6-7 he calls the law a dispensation of
death.

Thus Paul's view of death is extremely negative.
He sees it as something unnatural, something which
should not be part of human experience, and would not
be, if not for sin.

Alongside this negative view of death we also find
a positive attitude toward death in Paul, almost
exclusively connected with the death of Jesus. Thus
Paul says that Jesus' death was for others,[10] for sins
(Rom 4:25; 1 Cor 15:3) or sinners (Rom 5:6-8), for the
justification of others (Rom 5:9; Gal 2:21), for their
reconciliation with God (Rom 5:10; cf. Col 1:20, 22).

Paul has at least three distinct explanations of
how the death of Jesus benefits others.[11] First, he
can view Jesus' death as vicarious, a death which Jesus
endured in place of others, freeing them from sin and
death by taking on himself the punishment due their
sins. This is most explicit in Gal 3:10-13 (cf. also 2
Cor 5:21). Second, Paul can view Jesus' death as a
sacrifice, making reparation for sin and so setting
others free from it and its consequences. This

understanding is most explicit in Rom 3:23-6 (cf. also
1 Cor 5:7). Third, and most characteristically, Paul
can explain that the death of Jesus benefits others
when they are united with Jesus in his death and
resurrection.[12] The most extensive statement of this
view is found in Rom 6:3-11.

As Paul sees it, Jesus' death was an escape from
sin and death because death is an end to the dominion
of sin. Having paid its final penalty, one who has
died is free from sin; if that one should return to
life (as Jesus did), it would be a life no longer
dominated by sin (Rom 6:7-10). Through baptism the
believer dies with Christ and enters upon a new life
with him; the believer participates in Christ's escape
from sin and death (Rom 6:3-6, 11, 13). Death not only
ends subjection to sin, but also subjection to law (Rom
7:1-3). Thus dying with Christ is also escape from the
law (Rom 7:4, 6; 8:2). Because the law is so
intimately connected with sin, escape from sin requires
escape from the law (Rom 7:8).

Although the Christian has already died with
Christ, in Paul's view freedom from sin and death is
not complete. In Rom 6:3-5 he expresses this by saying
that the Christian has already entered upon a new life,
but that resurrection with Christ is still in the
future.[13] In other places Paul speaks of dying with
Christ as progressive rather than complete (2 Cor 4:10-
11; Phil 3:10-11).[14]

Thus Paul's belief as a Christian that the death
of Jesus was salvific leads him to give a very
different value to this death than to death in
general.[15] Paul can speak of death positively when the

death of something bad is in view (Rom 8:13).[16] But to
speak of the death of Jesus as good, and precisely
because his death overcomes death, involves Paul in a
paradox which is central to his understanding of
Christianity. And it is not only the death of Jesus
which is good, but also the union of Christians with
Jesus in his death.

It is striking however, that Paul's positive view
of the death of Christians seems to apply mainly to
what might be called their 'mystical' death in union
with Jesus, rather than to their literal death. Quite
possibly this is a result of Paul's expectation of the
imminent return of Jesus, giving him little occasion
for reflection on the literal death of Christians.
When Paul does refer to the literal death of
Christians, it is often in connection with hope for
resurrection from the dead (see above). As we have
observed, this context seems to imply a negative
attitude toward death. This attitude may be softened
somewhat in Paul's frequent references to the death of
Christians as 'falling asleep' (koimaomai),[17] which may
reflect Paul's hope for resurrection. However, even if
this is so, no real positive significance for death
itself is implied by the term.

Of the references to death which we have examined
so far, those in which Paul comes closest to giving a
positive significance to the literal death of
Christians are those in which he speaks of a
progressive dying with Christ (i.e., 2 Cor 4:10-11;
Phil 3:10-11). In these passages Paul says that
suffering is a way of entering more and more fully into
the death of Christ. He does not say that literal

death completes one's union with Jesus in his death, but this would be only a small step beyond what he does say. Such a view may underlie the unambiguous expression of a positive view of the literal death of Christians in one or two passages in Paul.

In Phil 1:21-4 Paul clearly expresses a positive attitude toward his own death, describing it as gain (kerdos - v 21) and saying that he has a desire (epithymia - v 23) to depart. Paul seems to explain the basis for his positive view of death when he refers to it as departing and being with Christ (v 23).[18] In view of his statement that for him to live is Christ (v 21), Paul cannot mean that death is the beginning of union with Christ. And since he hopes for resurrection from the dead, it seems unlikely that Paul here thinks of death as the completion of union with Christ. What is most likely is that Paul is thinking that his literal death will complete his union with Christ in his death. It is thus desirable as a step toward resurrection with Christ. As we have noted, Paul comes close to saying this explicitly in Phil 3:10-11.

Another passage in which this view comes to light is 2 Cor 5:1-10. Here Paul says that in our present condition we groan, longing (epipothountes - v 2) to put on our heavenly dwelling. But he goes on to make it clear that this does not mean death, but rather transformation (v 4), i.e., that which he describes at greater length in 1 Cor 15:51-5. He then speaks of being at home in the body as being away from the Lord and vice versa (v 6-8). Most immediately he seems to be contrasting untransformed and transformed human nature, since that is what he has just spoken about.

But it also possible that he is extrapolating from this a positive attitude toward death, on the grounds that our present condition has to go, one way or another, to allow full union with the Lord. If so, then this comes close to what Paul says in Phil 1:21-4 and suggests that what makes death desirable is that it is a step toward full union with Christ.[19]

Thus it appears that despite his extremely negative attitude toward death, Paul at times at least went so far as to desire it. The basis for this desire seems to have been the view that it was a step toward full union with Christ. This makes it seem likely that his desire for death is something that appeared only after Paul's conversion. Before his conversion his attitude toward death may have been entirely negative. One result of his conversion would then have been to change his attitude toward death, at least partly because as a follower of Jesus he had to see a positive value in the death of Jesus. And this in turn implied for Paul a positive value in the death of the Christian.

B.   The Cultural Context of Paul's View of Death

Although a negative view of death is probably a universal in human experience, the leading Greek and Roman views of death in the first century were less negative than that of Paul. The best summary of first-century Greek and Roman views of death is that of F. Cumont in _After Life in Roman Paganism_.[20] According to Cumont, the earliest Greek and Roman views of death regarded it as a transition to a shadowy, attenuated version of human life which followed upon death. At first this afterlife was seen as taking place in the tomb; later it was located in the nether world.[21] However, beginning in the second century BCE and extending into the first century CE, Greek philosophy, especially Epicureanism and Stoicism, was destructive of belief in after life. Epicurus argued that death was annihilation, but was not on that account to be feared, since non-existence precludes any possibility of suffering.[22] This view was adopted by other thinkers, but also gained some currency among people generally, as is shown by its expression in epitaphs. One such epitaph was so common that it is sometimes expressed only in initials: I was not; I was; I am not; I do not care (Non fui, fui, non sum, non curo). According to the Stoics, at death the human soul was re-united with the fiery first principle, penetrating the universe, of which the soul was a part. For many Stoics, this amounted to personal annihilation; thus they could quote Epicurus approvingly (cf. Seneca, Ep. Mor. 24.18; 36.9). The currency of Stoic views is also shown by their expression in epitaphs.[23] The Stoics argued that the only true evil is moral evil; since death is not a moral evil, it is not an evil at all, and the wise person will train him or herself to see it this way.[24] Part of this training is anticipation of one's own death[25] and that of others (Epictetus 3.24.88).[26]

According to Cumont, this was only one strand of first-century Greek and Roman thinking about death. The first century BCE saw the rebirth of belief in the immortality of the soul. This belief had come to classical expression in the philosophy of Plato in the fourth century BCE, but had then declined until being

revived in the first century, especially by Neo-
Pythagoreans. According to this view death was the
transition to a new kind of life, different from, but
not inferior to, the life which preceded death. Under
the influence of Posidonius, according to Cumont, even
Stoics like Cicero and Seneca embraced this belief.
This belief underlay the popular mystery cults.[27]

As we have seen, Paul understands death as a
consequence of sin and thus as something unnatural.
The Stoics and Epicureans regarded death as natural and
consequently not as an evil. They recognize that human
beings spontaneously consider death the ultimate
misfortune, but argue that this is not the real truth
of the matter and that we must strive to see death as
it really is. For the Stoics and Epicureans death was
at worst something indifferent. For those who believed
in the immortality of the soul, death took its
character from what followed it. Those who expected to
enter into a blessed state at death could regard it
positively; those who did not, could not. But even in
the latter case, it is not death itself which is the
negative quantity, but rather life after death.

The spectrum of Jewish views concerning death was
similar to that of Greek and Roman views (with one
significant exception) and thus also less negative than
Paul's view.[28] The oldest Jewish view, reflected
throughout much of the Hebrew scripture, was like the
earliest Greek and Roman view: death was the
transition to a shadowy existence either in the tomb or
in Sheol.[29] In the book of Ecclesiastes we find a view
of death which is similar to that of the Epicureans and
Stoics, i.e., that death is annihilation (cf. Eccl

3:18-22; 9:4-6). This may also have been the view of
the first-century Sadducees.[30] In first-century
Judaism we also find the view that the soul is immortal
and thus that death is the beginning of a new kind of
life. This view is expressed clearly in the Wisdom of
Solomon and the writings of Philo of Alexandria; Philo
is obviously influenced by Greek philosophy.[31]

Alongside these views of death which correspond to
those of Greeks and Romans, we also find among first-
century Jews a distinctive view of death, i.e., that
which is implied in expectation of resurrection from
the dead. This expectation developed in apocalyptic
circles in Judaism and was first expressed in the book
of Daniel. It was embraced by the first-century
Pharisees and is expressed in the later rabbinic
writings.[32] As we have already noted in discussing
Paul's view of death, hope for resurrection, in effect
a hope for the reversal of death, implies a negative
view of death. Death is not indifferent or the
transition to a new form of existence; it is an evil
which must be overcome. This is a much more negative
view of death than the Greek and Roman views, or the
other Jewish views, which we have briefly examined.
And it is identical to one element of Paul's negative
view of death.

Even more importantly than this however, we also
find in the Judaism contemporary with Paul the view
that death is a result of sin and is thus unnatural.
This view of death is most closely connected with the
apocalyptic circles which hoped for resurrection from
the dead. But we also find it in combination with the
view that the soul is immortal in the Wisdom of

Solomon.   In the book of Wisdom we read, "God created
man for incorruption...but through the devil's envy
death entered the world" (2:23-4; cf. 1:13).[33]   In
passages like 2 Apoc. Bar. 54:15, 19 it is clear that
death is the result both of the first sin and of the
subsequent sins of individuals, which is also Paul's
view in Rom 5:12.   It seems likely that Paul's
understanding of death as a result of sin and thus as
something unnatural, as well as his expectation of
resurrection from the dead, is derived from these
streams of contemporary Jewish thought.[34]

Paul's view of Jesus' death as one which benefits
others is not found outside of Christian circles, but
the ways in which he explains how this can be, do have
parallels in his environment.   His views of Jesus'
death as vicarious and as sacrificial, two ideas which
are closely related, make use of perspectives on death
familiar to Jews, Greeks and Romans.   Sacrifice (though
not of human beings, of course) was a central element
of the cults both of the God of Israel and of the many
gods worshipped in the Greco-Roman world.[35]   And that
the death of a person might be vicarious or sacrificial
in the broad sense of being for their benefit, was also
a common idea.[36]   Paul's most characteristic view of
the death of Jesus as one in which believers are united
with him, also has at least distant parallels in some
of the mystery cults.   Although it is not clear that
any of the mysteries involved union with a god or
goddess who had died and returned to life, the central
figures of many of these cults had died and returned to
life (e.g., Persephone, Dionysius, Osiris) and
participation in the mystery was intended somehow to

assure the participant of a blessed existence after death.[37]

Within Christian circles Paul may have been the originator of the view that Jesus' death benefits the believer in that the believer is united with Jesus in his death. But he was certainly not the first to see Jesus' death as sacrificial. He undoubtedly adopted this understanding of Jesus' death from those who were Christians before him.

Naturally there is no parallel to Paul's positive view of the death of Christians as a participation in the death of Jesus outside of Christian circles. However, speaking of death as 'falling asleep' is not unique to Paul and is especially common among Jews who shared his hope for resurrection of the dead.[38] And among both Jews and Gentiles we do find positive views of death which have some other basis than participation in the death of Jesus.

First of all, the Stoics took a positive view of death because of its intrinsic indifference. Because death was a natural and inevitable part of life, the Stoics considered that one might end one's life if one chose to do so, in order to secure release from painful circumstances.[39] Seneca even goes so far as to say that "death is so little to be feared that through its good office nothing is to be feared" (Ep. Mor. 24.11; cf. 4.3).[40]

Of course, this Stoic view is one which human beings have probably always adopted spontaneously, without any philosophical basis, when life became sufficiently difficult.[41] But the Stoics at times went beyond mere acceptance of death as a way out of

difficulties. Their view of death was so positive that
the Stoics had to counsel against excessive attraction
to suicide. Musonius Rufus says "One who by living is
of use to many does not have the right to choose to die
unless by dying he may be of use to more."[42] And
Seneca warns against craving death, a lust for death
(libido moriendi) which can overtake anyone (Ep. Mor.
24.22-6).

Secondly, some first-century Jews took a positive
view of death on the basis that the soul is immortal
and survives death. Plato had argued that the soul was
intrinsically immortal. His position seems to have had
little influence on first-century Greco-Roman
philosophy, but it was taken up by Hellenistic Jews.
The book of Wisdom regards the souls of the righteous
as immortal (cf. 3:1-6). And Philo continues the views
of Plato even more fully. Because the soul is
immortal, death is no disaster, but rather entry into
an even more blessed state than human life before
death.

Among Christians Paul's positive view of death on
the basis of Jesus' death is more moderate than some,
notably that of Ignatius of Antioch. In the letters
written as he was being taken to Rome to be executed,
he expresses a longing for death far stronger than
anything we find in the letters of Paul. In Eph. 1.2
he refers to fighting with beasts at Rome as a
privilege, and in Trall. 10 he says that he longs to
fight with the beasts because of the reality of Jesus'
suffering (cf. Smyr. 3.2;. 4.2). But this longing is
most evident in his letter to the church at Rome, which
he begs not to try to prevent his death.[43] He says "It

is better for me to die in Christ Jesus than to be king....Hinder me not from living, do not wish me to die....Suffer me to follow the example of the passion" (<u>Rom.</u> 6.1-3). He anticipates that he may be less eager to die when the time comes nearer and asks the Romans not to heed him then, "Even though when I come I beseech you myself, do not be persuaded by me, but rather obey this, which I write to you....In the midst of life I write to you desiring death (<u>eron</u> <u>tou</u> <u>apothanein</u>)" (<u>Rom.</u> 7.2).

C. Psychological Analysis of Paul's View of Death

Paul's negative view of death is similar to the view which all human beings share, and so requires no special explanation beyond that which would apply to human beings generally. Paul's view that death is a result of sin and consequently not a natural part of human existence is more negative than some views of death. But as we have seen, Paul probably takes this view over from certain streams of contemporary Jewish thought. If so, then this too requires no special explanation beyond that which would apply to this sector of first-century Judaism.

Paul's positive view of the death of Christians as a participation in the death of Jesus does seem to require psychological analysis. It is true that others in Paul's day also had a positive view of death; we have discussed the positive view of death found in some first-century Jewish writings, based on the idea that the soul is immortal, and the Stoic idea that one has the right to end one's life if circumstances require it, since this is only to anticipate nature. But

Paul's positive view of death has a completely
different basis, i.e., the participation of the
Christian in the death and resurrection of Jesus;
consequently it does not seem possible to explain it as
adoption of a view current in his cultural milieu.

The most important psychological explanation of a
positive view of death so far proposed is that of S.
Freud.   Freud argued that human life is propelled by
two basic instincts - the erotic instinct and the death
instinct.   The aim of the former is to establish ever
greater unities and to preserve them; the aim of the
latter is to undo connections and so to destroy things.
Neither exists in isolation; the two instincts are
fused in varying proportions in all instinctual
manifestations.   Freud argued that the death of the
individual is the final accomplishment of the death
instinct (except, presumably, in the case of certain
completely unexpected accidental deaths and
killings).[44]

In the earliest stage of life, both the erotic
instinct and the death instinct are focused on oneself.
In the course of development both are turned outward
toward objects other than oneself.   But if they must be
withdrawn from these objects, the instinctual energy is
again directed toward oneself.   Resolution of the
Oedipus complex is a key instance of this.   When the
child abandons his or her aggressive desire to
eliminate the parent of his or her own sex by
identifying with that parent, the aggressive energy
formerly directed against the parent becomes available
to the superego to be used against the ego.[45]   Later
abandonments of aggressive energy directed outward may

result in a further increase of such energy available
to the superego. In any case this energy is refocused
on oneself. Thus Freud says that it is necessary for
us to destroy some other person or thing so as not to
destroy ourselves.[46]

In light of these theories, we may suggest that
Paul's positive view of death has three sources. First
of all, it is a result of an increase in the difficulty
of his life. This is clear in the case of what he says
in Phil 1:21-4; immediately before making these
comments Paul has described his imprisonment (1:7, 12-
14) and some obscure hostility toward him on the part
of other Christians (1:15-18). The same thing is
probably the case with regard to what Paul says in 2
Cor 5:1-10. Earlier in this letter too he has spoken
about various afflictions.[47]

Secondly, Paul's positive view of death is a
result of his having an understanding of Christian life
as a participation in the death and resurrection of
Jesus, which provides a conceptual framework within
which it is possible to view death positively. Thus I
am suggesting that when the difficulty of Paul's life
increased, inclining him to think of death as an escape
from its sufferings (as is probably the universal
tendency of human beings), his understanding of
Christian life gave him a way to follow that
inclination.

But thirdly, we can suppose that psychological
factors were involved, specifically an increase in the
strength of the aggressive impulses which Paul directed
against himself. Before his conversion Paul had the
extremely negative view of death characteristic of

apocalyptic Judaism, and his aggressive impulses were directed strongly outward, taking the form of competition and boasting and even persecution of Christians. As we have seen, Paul's conversion meant an attempt to abandon this outward direction of aggression. We have also seen that Paul failed to carry this out completely; still his conversion entailed a significant reduction in the direction of his aggressive energy toward others. And if Freud is right, this brought with it an increase in aggressive energy directed toward himself, located in the superego or elsewhere. This then would be the source of his inclination toward death.

We may see a parallel to this in Stoic philosophy. It seems likely that the desire for death which can be seen in some Stoics results from the Stoic attempt to extirpate all passions of every kind. This might easily produce an inner-directed aggression of the superego which would manifest itself in lust for death. Likewise the Epicurean openness to death can be seen as a result of their quest for ataraxia.

Likewise, Ignatius of Antioch, taking his cue from Paul, is critical of competition and boasting in himself and others. Adopting this attitude from Paul, but without Paul's personality structure, could easily lead to a desire for death much greater than Paul's own.

Notes

[1]Rom 8:38; 14:7-9; 1 Cor 3:22; 7:39; 15:6; 2 Cor 7:3; cf. 2 Tim 4:1.

[2]On Paul's view of death see C. Clifton Black, "Pauline Perspectives on Death in Romans 5-8," JBL 103 (1984) 413-33.

[3]Rom 1:29; 11:3; 13:9; 1 Thess 2:15.

[4]Rom 7:24; 8:36; 1 Cor 9:15; 15:26; 2 Cor 1:9-10; 2:16; 6:9; 11:23; Phil 2:8, 27, 30.

[5]Rom 1:4; 4:17, 24; 8:11, 34; 10:7, 9; 11:15; 14:9; 1 Cor 11:26; 15:3-4, 12-57; 2 Cor 1:9; 5:15; Gal 1:1; 1 Thess 1:10; 4:13-18; cf. Eph 1:20; 5:14; Col 1:18.

[6]Rom 4:19; 1 Cor 15:31; 2 Cor 7:10; cf. 1 Tim 5:6.

[7]On this see R. Bultmann, Theology of the NT, trans. by K. Grobel (New York: Scribner, 1951) 1.246-9; J. C. Beker, Paul the Apostle: The Triumph of God in Life and Thought (Philadelphia: Fortress, 1980) 213-34.

[8]Cf. also Rom 6:16; 7:23-4; 8:6, 10, 13; and Eph 2:1, 5; Col 2:13.

[9]Cf. Bultmann, Theology, 1.259-69; Beker, Paul the Apostle, 235-54.

[10]Rom 14:15; 1 Cor 8:11; 2 Cor 5:14-15; 1 Thess 5:10; cf. Eph 5:2, 25.

[11]Cf. R. Bultmann, Theology, 1.295-300; H. Ridderbos, Paul: An Outline of His Theology, trans. by J. R. DeWitt (Grand Rapids, MI: Eerdmans, 1975) 186-93, 206-14.

[12]On this see R. Tannehill, Dying and Rising with Christ: A Study in Pauline Theology (BZNW 32; Berlin: Töpelmann, 1967) and E. Schweizer, "Dying and Rising with Christ," NTS 14 (1967) 1-14.

[13]Cf. 2 Tim 2:11.

[14]In Eph 2:5-6; Col 2:12-13; 2:20-3:1 it is said that the Christian has already risen with Christ, but there remains an eschatological reservation (Eph 2:7; Col 3:3-4).

[15]Cf. Eph 2:14-16.

[16]Cf. Col 3:5; 2 Thess 2:8.

[17]1 Cor 7:39; 11:30; 15:6, 18, 20, 51; 1 Thess 4:13-18.

[18]A. J. Droge argues that in Phil 1:21-6 Paul expresses a positive attitude toward suicide ("Mori lucrum: Paul and Ancient Theories of Suicide," NovT 30 (1988) 263-86, especially pp 278-85).

[19]For this interpretation of the passage see C. K. Barrett, The Second Epistle to the Corinthians (HNTC; New York: Harper and Row, 1973) 157-9. V. P. Furnish (II Corinthians [AB 32A; Garden City, NY: Doubleday, 1984] 301-3) does not see the thought of v 6-8 as comparable to that of Phil 1:21-4. J. Murphy-O'Connor has taken Furnish's argument one step further by arguing that in 2 Cor 5:6b Paul quotes a Corinthian slogan which Paul then corrects ("'Being at Home in the Body We Are in Exile from the Lord' (2 Cor 5:6b)," RB 93 (1986) 214-21.

[20]F. Cumont, After Life in Roman Paganism (Silliman Memorial Lectures; New Haven: Yale, 1922). See also E. Rohde, Psyche: The Cult of Souls and Belief in Immortality Among the Greeks trans. by W. B. Hillis (New York: Harcourt, Brace, 1925) [original publication 1897]; R. Lane Fox, Pagans and Christians (New York: Knopf, 1987) 95-8; R. Bultmann, "thanatos ktl.," TDNT 3.8-13; L. E. Keck, "New Testament Views of Death," Perspectives on Death ed. by L. O. Mills (Nashville and New York: Abingdon, 1969) 50-61; A. Toynbee, "Traditional Attitudes Toward Death," in A. Toynbee et al., Man's Concern with Death (St. Louis, New York, San Francisco: McGraw-Hill, 1969) 59-94; G. J. Gruman, "Ethics of Death and Dying: Historical Perspective," Omega 9 (1978-9) 203-37; and Black, "Pauline Perspectives on Death," 414-19. J. E. Phillips surveys the spectrum of Greco-Roman attitudes toward death as she discusses the consolation of death and bereavement in classical literature, and Plutarch's place in this tradition in H. Martin, Jr. and J. E. Phillips, "Consolatio ad Uxorem (Moralia 608 A - 612 B)," Plutarch's Ethical Writings and Early Christian Literature ed. by H. D. Betz (SCHNT 4; Leiden: Brill, 1978) 397-412. For a history of attitudes toward death (though it does not include the first century) see P. Ariès, The Hour of Our Death trans. by H. Weaver (New York: Knopf, 1981). His argument is presented more briefly in P. Ariès, Western Attitudes Toward Death:

From the Middle Ages to the Present trans. by P. M.
Ranum (The Johns Hopkins Symposia in Comparative
History; Baltimore: Johns Hopkins, 1974).

[21]Cumont, After Life, 3-5, 44-90.

[22]Epicurus,   Epistle   to   Menoeceus   in   Diogenes
Laertius, Lives 10.124-6; Hai Kyriai 2 in Diogenes
Laertius, Lives 10.139.   Cf. also Lucretius, de Rer.
Nat. 3.830-1094.   Diogenes Laertius also attributes
this view to Diogenes the Cynic.   He reports that when
Diogenes was asked if death was evil, he replied by
asking how it could be evil since when it is present,
we are not aware of it (Lives 6.68).

[23]Cumont, After Life, 5-20.

[24]Musonius Rufus,   "On Training,"   in   C. E. Lutz,
Musonius Rufus "The Roman Socrates" (Yale Classical
Studies 10; New Haven: Yale, 1947) 52-7 (cf. also pp.
62-3,   74-7,   110-11);   Epictetus   1.27.7;   2.1.13-20;
3.3.15; 3.26.38-9; Seneca, Ep. Mor. 4; 23; 24; 30.

[25]Musonius Rufus (Lutz, Musonius Rufus, 131).   Cf.
Epictetus, Ench. 21 and Seneca, Ep. Mor. 12; 26.

[26]For a recent discussion of this see R. MacMullen,
Paganism in the Roman Empire (New Haven and London:
Yale, 1981) 62-73.   MacMullen is uncertain about the
currency of Epicurean and Stoic views among the general
populace.

[27]Cumont, After Life, 20-40, 91-127; cf. also Lane
Fox, Pagans and Christians, 96-7.   MacMullen (Paganism,
53-7) doubts that belief in immortality was prominent
in Greco-Roman religion, even in the mystery cults.

[28]On Jewish views of death see G. F. Moore, Judaism
in the First Centuries of the Christian Era.   The Age
of the Tannaim (New York: Schocken, 1971) 2.287-322
[original publication 1927, 1930]; G. von Rad, "zao
ktl. B. 2:   Death in the OT," TDNT 2.846-9; R.
Bultmann, "zao ktl. D: The Concept of Life in
Judaism," TDNT 2.855-61; R. Martin-Achard, From Death
to Life: A Study of the Development of the Doctrine of
the Resurrection in the Old Testament trans. by J. P.
Smith (Edinburgh and London: Oliver and Boyd, 1960);
L. H. Silberman, "Death in the Hebrew Bible and
Apocalyptic Literature," Perspectives on Death, 13-32;
G. W. E. Nickelsburg, Jr., Resurrection, Immortality

and Eternal Life in Intertestamental Judaism (HTS 26;
Cambridge, MA: Harvard, 1972); P. A. Robinson, The
Conception of Death in Judaism in the Hellenistic and
Early Roman Period (Univeristy of Wisconsin - Madison
dissertation, 1978); and P. Perkins, Resurrection: New
Testament Witness and Contemporary Reflection (Garden
City, NY: Doubleday, 1984) 37-69.

[29]Moore, Judaism, 2.287-92.

[30]Cf. Josephus, J. W., 2.165; Ant. 18.16; Mark
12:18-27 and parallels; Acts 23:8.

[31]Moore, Judaism, 2.292-5; Perkins, Resurrection,
51-5.

[32]Moore, Judaism, 2.295-311, 379-95; Perkins,
Resurrection, 37-51.

[33]Cf. also 2 Enoch 30.17; Apoc. Mos. 14; 4 Ezra
3.7, 21f, 26; 2 Apoc. Bar. 23.4; 56.6. This view is
also found in the later rabbinic literature (cf. Sipre
Deut. 323; Gen. Rab. 16.6; b. Sabb. 55).

[34]E. Käsemann, Commentary on Romans trans. by G. W.
Bromiley (Grand Rapids, MI: Eerdmans, 1980) 148.

[35]On this see R. K. Yerkes, Sacrifice in Greek and
Roman Religions and Early Judaism (Hale Lectures; New
York: Scribner, 1952).

[36]See S. K. Williams, Jesus' Death as Saving Event:
The Background and Origin of a Concept (HDR 2;
Missoula, MT: Scholars, 1975) 91-163; M. Hengel, The
Atonement: The Origins of the Doctrine in the NT
trans. by J. Bowden (Philadelphia: Fortress, 1981) 4-
32.

[37]For a statement of the similarity between Paul's
understanding of dying and rising with Christ and the
ideology of the mystery religions, see Bultmann,
Theology 1.298. More recently A. J. M. Wedderburn has
emphasized their dissimilarity ("The Soteriology of the
Mysteries and Pauline Baptismal Theology," NovT 29
[1987] 53-72). Though Wedderburn's argument is cogent
and eliminates the possibility that Paul's idea derives
from mystery religion, there remains an undeniable
element of similarity between the two (cf. W. A. Meeks,
The First Urban Christians: The Social World of the

Apostle Paul [New Haven and London: Yale, 1983] 241-2,
n. 44).

[38]On this see O. Michel, "Zur Lehre vom
Todesschlaf," ZNW 35 (1936) 285-90; J. G. S. S.
Thompson, "Sleep: An Aspect of Jewish Anthropology,"
VT 5 (1955) 421-33; and R. E. Bailey, "Is 'Sleep' the
Proper Biblical Term for the Intermediate State?" ZNW
55 (1964) 161-7.

[39]Musonius Rufus (Lutz, Musonius Rufus, 133);
Epictetus 2.1.20; 4.1.108; Seneca, Ep. Mor. 17.5-7, 9;
Pliny. Epist. 1.12, 22; 3.7, 16.

[40]On the Stoic view of suicide see A. J. Droge,
"Mori lucrum: Paul and Ancient Theories of Suicide,"
especially pp 268-73.   Droge argues that in the ancient
world, Greeks in general, as well as Jews, and
Christians prior to Augustine, saw suicide as justified
in at least some circumstances.

[41]For a discussion of the Greek commonplace that
death is a gain for those whose life is a burden see D.
W. Palmer, "'To Die is Gain' (Philippians i 21)," NovT
17 (1975) 203-18.

[42]Lutz, Musonius Rufus, 133.

[43]Rom. 2.2; 4.1-2; 5.2, 3; 8.1.

[44]Freud first developed the concept of a death
instinct in Beyond the Pleasure Principle, reprinted in
The Standard Edition of the Complete Psychological
Works of Sigmund Freud ed. by J. Strachey (London:
Hogarth, 1964) 18.1-64.   In later discussions (e.g.,
"Anxiety and Instinctual Life," New Introductory
Lectures on Psychoanalysis, reprinted in Standard
Edition 22.81-111 (see especially pp. 103-11), Freud
also referred to this as the aggressive instinct; this
is the form in which contemporary psychoanalysis speaks
of this instinct; see C. Brenner, An Elementary
Textbook of Psychoanalysis.   Revised Edition (Garden
City, NY: Doubleday, 1974) 19-21.   For a critical
discussion of Freud's death instinct see E. Fromm, The
Anatomy of Human Destructiveness (New York, Chicago,
San Francisco: Holt, Rinehart and Winston, 1973) 439-
78.   One of Fromm's alternative explanations of human
destructiveness is what he calls necrophilia.   Fromm
seems to regard necrophilia as responsible for

destruction both of self and others (<u>Ibid</u>., 364), but he has little to say about the former.

[45]Brenner, <u>An</u> <u>Elementary</u> <u>Textbook</u> <u>of</u> <u>Psycho-analysis</u>, 117-18.

[46]"Anxiety and Instinctual Life," <u>New</u> <u>Introductory</u> <u>Lectures</u> <u>on</u> <u>Psychoanalysis</u>, <u>Standard</u> <u>Edition</u> 22.105.

[47]Cf. 4:8-10; 1:3-11.   In the case of the latter passage Paul is clearly speaking about recent experience; however, some consider this part of a different letter than that which contains 5:1-10.

Chapter 6

Conclusion

On the basis of the foregoing investigations into the topics of competition and boasting, sexuality, parent and child, and death in Paul, we may now draw two sorts of conclusions. First, we may tentatively sketch out a synthesis of Paul's personality as it has been revealed by these investigations. And second, we may consider the impact of these investigations on the interpretation of Paul's letters.[1]

A. Paul's Personality

All of these investigations have confirmed in various ways that Paul's conversion to Jesus marked a psychological turning point in his life, as well as a turning point in other ways. Though there is considerable continuity between the pre- and post-conversion periods of Paul's life, his conversion modified his personality in important ways.

As we have seen, before his conversion Paul was competitive and boastful. He also had a negative attitude toward sexuality and favored celibacy. His attitude toward parents and children was largely positive, but he also had negative feelings about parents and children which were largely unconscious. And he had a very negative view of death, regarding it as unnatural and the ultimate evil in human life.

Many of these traits he shared with others in his cultural milieu. Competition and boasting and ambivalence about the parent-child relationship are very common in Paul's cultural context. And his view of death corresponds closely to apocalyptic streams of contemporary Judaism. The trait in which Paul differs most from his contemporaries (though he is hardly unique in this) is his negative attitude toward sexuality. As we have seen, this can be readily explained as a result of the formation of an unusually strong prohibition of sexuality by Paul's superego in the course of his resolution of the Oedipus complex.

This view of Paul is compatible with the other elements of his personality which we have observed. It is most compatible with Paul's largely unconscious ambivalence about his relationship with his parents. The formation of the superego always involves some repression of negative feelings about parents as the child identifies with them in giving up incestuous wishes. An unusually strong superego would entail an unusually complete repression of negative feelings about parents, which may be what we see in Paul. Likewise a strong superego could easily underlie competition and boasting; this could occur in two different ways. First, competition and boasting might be understood as a sublimation of the sexual drive denied by Paul's superego. Second, an unusually strong superego could result in great effort to achieve,[2] and might easily lead to competition and boasting of one's success. And if competition is seen as direction of the aggressive impulses outward, this is also compatible with an extremely negative attitude toward death since it involves rejection of aggressive impulses as directed toward oneself.

That Paul shares these traits with others is not surprising if, as psychoanalytic theory claims, the Oedipus complex is universal. Formation of the superego in the course of resolving the Oedipus complex might easily produce similar traits in many of Paul's contemporaries. However, Paul's unusually negative attitude toward sexuality suggests that his superego may have been stronger, more in control of him, than was the case for others in his day. This is suggested even more strongly by Paul's persecution of the followers of Jesus. We might speculate that in order to escape the aggressive energy directed at him by his own superego, Paul projected onto the Christians whatever it was in him which elicited his superego's condemnation, and thus persecuted them in place of himself. Theissen argues that Paul projected his own unconscious conflict with the law onto the Christians.[3]

Thus the picture of Paul that emerges from all of these observations is that of a man dominated by his superego. In resolving his Oedipus complex, he repressed his negative feelings about his parents almost completely, identified strongly with them, and strove throughout his life to live up to the ideals that were thus implanted in him, above all by attempting to surpass others. This unconscious identification with his parents and direction of his aggressive impulses outward in the form of competition, led him to identify unconsciously with God and to direct his aggressive impulses outward in the form of persecution.

His conversion modified this picture decisively. In his conversion Paul became convinced that God had raised Jesus and that the Christians were right in their understanding of what fidelity to God now required. His encounter with the risen Jesus showed Paul that the entire direction of his life, which had made him a persecutor, was wrong. What he had done in an effort to surpass others as a servant of God proved to be something which made him least among God's servants. Psychologically, as we have seen, this meant a change in Paul's identity; he exchanged the identity of one zealous for the traditions of the fathers for the identity of follower and apostle of Jesus. And in large measure this was the result of a new identification which modified Paul's superego. His superego was formed through identification with his parents and subsequently strengthened by an identification with God. But in his conversion Paul identified with Jesus and with God as revealed in Jesus. And this identification seems to have symbolized for Paul some measure of independence for the ego vis-a-vis the superego. Identification with Jesus meant release from complete domination of ego by superego. And at the same time this reduced the opposition between Paul's ego and his instinctual impulses, i.e., the id.[4]

Of course, Paul does not use this terminology. But it is clear that his conversion meant a new awareness of himself, one in which he is critical of precisely those things which before his conversion were a source of pride. As Theissen has argued, Paul comes closest to an explicit discussion of the part played by his id and superego in his going astray, in Romans 7. In v 23 he says that another law in his members (heteron nomon en tois melesin mou) is at war with the

law of his mind (to nomo tou noos mou) and takes him
(me) captive. Theissen plausibly contends that the
first of these corresponds closely to the id, the
second to the superego, and the third to the ego.
Faith in Christ is the means by which conflict between
id and superego, which leads to captivity for the ego,
is overcome.[5]

Paul's formulation in v 23, and for that matter
the whole argument of v 14-25, seems to lay the greater
blame for the captivity of the ego on the id, which
overpowers the superego and makes its agreement with
the law ineffective. Earlier however, in v 7-13, Paul
has suggested that it is the superego, in its embrace
of the law, which has aroused the power of the id.
Thus id and superego are correlative, neither operative
in isolation from the other. However, it seems that
for Paul, the impact of his conversion on his superego
is the more obvious and important.

The greatest and most obvious effect of this
reduction of the power of Paul's superego as a result
of his conversion, is his opposition to competition and
boasting. But the undermining of Paul's superego also
affected other attitudes. As we have seen above,
becoming a Christian meant a gradual modification of
Paul's view of sexuality. Unless Paul himself wrote
Ephesians, this modification never became fully
conscious as far as we know. But there are indications
that Paul was moving toward a more positive view of
sexuality, and I suggest that, psychologically, this
was a result of the modification of his superego and
its prohibition of sexuality. Similarly, becoming a
Christian seems to have meant growth in Paul's ability

to recognize a negative dimension to the parent-child relationship, at least as it applied to God the Father and his son Jesus. Psychologically this can be seen as a result of the lessening of the power of his superego and the repression of negative feelings about his parents.

However, despite the reduction in the power of Paul's superego brought about by his conversion, his superego remained strong. His conversion was a modification of his psychological make-up, not a complete transformation of it. This is indicated already by the continuation of his negative attitude toward sexuality and his positive attitude toward parents, despite the modifications introduced by his conversion. But this is even more strongly indicated by the fact that despite his opposition to competition and boasting, Paul remained competitive and boastful, i.e., remained driven by his superego. As we have seen, Paul was partly unconscious of this. But he was also partly conscious of it, and was able to reconcile it with his view that competition and boasting were excluded for the Christian. He did so mainly by means of a conscious identification with God as revealed to Paul by his conversion.

Another indication of the continuing strength of Paul's superego is his development of a positive attitude toward death as a Christian. This can be understood psychologically as a result of the partial diversion of Paul's aggressive impulses from external expression in competition and boasting, and the complete abandonment of their expression in persecution. This resulted in their being turned inward against Paul himself, quite possibly through the agency of the superego. The conscious manifestation of this was an openness to death.

It is important to realize that with regard to its effects on some of the issues we have been discussing, Paul's conversion can be seen as a conversion toward, not away from, Judaism. Paul's pre-conversion competition and boastfulness, and his negativity toward sexuality, were more characteristic of first-century Gentiles than of Jews. And the modification of these traits by his conversion brought Paul into closer conformity with contemporary Jews. Jews and Gentiles do not seem to differ markedly in their attitudes toward parents and children. But at least we can say that in allowing Paul to come to terms with the Akedah, his conversion brought him closer to contemporary Jews. It is only in Paul's pre-Christian view of death that he was characteristically Jewish. But even in this case, his conversion brought him to a view which was similar to that of some other Jews.

Finally, it may be helpful to indicate briefly what this analysis suggests about categorizing Paul's personality according to various typological systems. It may first of all be worthy of note that there was developing in Paul's own day a typology of personalities, each determined by the predominance of one of four humors in the body: thus the sanguine, choleric, phlegmatic and melancholic personalities.[6] On the basis of the portrait developed above, Paul would probably be classified as a choleric person.

Freudian psychology speaks of oral, anal and phallic personality types. The first is characterized by self-assurance, optimism and generosity, as well as their opposites. The second is characterized by orderliness, parsimony and stubbornness, and their opposites. And the phallic personality is characterized by ambition and a need for recognition and applause.[7] Paul seems to be an example of the phallic personality.

Jungian psychology divides people into introverts and extraverts, and further in terms of their primary and secondary preferences for sensation, intuition, feeling and thinking. There are sixteen different possible combinations of these categories.[8] In these terms Paul seems to be an extravert with a strong preference for feeling and a secondary preference for intuition. Such a person is characterized by sensitivity to praise and criticism, perseverance, idealism, and loyalty, as well as other qualities.[9]

At the conclusion of this sort of analysis of Paul, we need to step back and realize that it was Paul's strong, severe superego, modified by his conversion, which made him the amazingly energetic and productive person he was. Not all of the elements of his personality which we have observed seem equally good. We might wish that Paul was less competitive and boastful, that he had a less negative view of sexuality, a more complete awareness of the ambivalence of parent and child, a less extreme attitude toward death. But all of these are parts of a whole which was tremendously successful by any measure. Paul was successful because of his drive to succeed, which also underlies these other elements. And in addition to the accomplishments of his activities, Paul's psychological make-up also contributed to his ability to express an understanding of Christianity which has remained meaningful for 2000 years. Awareness of the psychological background of his letters may help to make them even more meaningful today than they otherwise would be.

B. The Interpretation of Paul's Letters

The main impact of psychological analysis of Paul on the interpretation of his letters is that it allows us to understand certain contradictions, i.e., between condemnation of competition and boasting and continuing to do these things, and between positive and negative attitudes toward sexuality, the parent-child relationship and death. Psychological analysis allows us to understand these contradictions as tensions between conscious and less conscious attitudes.

Even more important than this, however, is the possibility opened up by psychological interpretation for seeing these contradictions as tensions between attitudes Paul is in the process of leaving behind and attitudes he is moving toward. With regard to competition and boasting, Paul's conscious opposition to these traits is the direction of his development; his unconscious continuing to compete and boast is what he is leaving behind. With regard to the other three topics, I have suggested that his conscious attitude is the one which he is in the process of leaving behind, and his unconscious attitude represents the direction of growth. Thus Paul is moving away from his negative attitude toward sexuality, his simple positive attitude toward parents and his extremely negative attitude toward death. And he is moving toward a more positive appreciation of sexuality, awareness of ambivalence toward parents and a less negative attitude toward death.

Situating Paul's attitudes on these topics within this developmental framework has two important consequences for our understanding of his thought. First, seeing some of these attitudes as ones he is in the process of leaving behind leads us to minimize their significance as elements of Paul's thought. Thus we see that Paul's competition and boasting, negative attitude toward sexuality, etc. are not as important as their opposites, considered as elements of Paul's theology. Second, seeing others of these attitudes as ones Paul is moving toward puts them in a helpful context. When we see Paul's opposition to competition and boasting as the reversal of an established tendency to the contrary in himself, we do not so easily absolutize it as we otherwise might. And when we see his positive attitude toward sexuality and death, and recognition of ambivalence toward parents as attitudes which are slowly gestating in him, we can understand why he does not develop these thoughts more fully.

In addition, perceiving the direction of development of Paul's personality and his thought allows us to extrapolate what might be a further development of his thought more reliably than would otherwise be possible.

Notes

[1]On this topic see A. Vanhoye, "Personnalité de Paul et exégèse paulinienne," L'Apotre Paul: Personnalité, Style et Conception du Ministère ed. by A. Vanhoye (Leuven: University Press, 1986) 3-15.

[2]On the superego as the bearer of the ego ideal see S. Freud, "The Dissection of the Psychical Personality," New Introductory Lectures on Psychoanalysis, reprinted in The Standard Edition of the Complete Psychological Works of Sigmund Freud ed. by J. Strachey (London: Hogarth, 1964) 22.64-7.

[3]G. Theissen, Psychological Aspects of Pauline Theology trans. by J. P. Galvin (Philadelphia: Fortress, 1987) 234-43. In making this argument Theissen rejects the view that Paul persecuted the Christians in an effort to secure esteem and influence within Judaism. However, it does not seem necessary to choose between the two. As I suggest above, Paul's superego might have brought him to the point of persecution both in order to fulfill his ego ideal and, by means of projection, to evade the aggression of his superego toward himself.

[4]On identification and identity see E. Erikson, Identity: Youth and Crisis (New York: Norton, 1968) 155-65.

[5]Theissen, Psychological Aspects, 244-50. Theissen cites G. Créspy, "Exégèse et psychoanalyse. Considerations aventueuses sur Romains 7,7-25," L'evangile, hier et aujourd'hui. Mélanges offerts au Prof. Franz-J. Leenhardt (Geneva: Labor et Fides, 1968) 169-79; A. Vergote, "Der Beitrag der Psychoanalyse zur Exegese. Leben, Gesetz und Ich-Spaltung im 7. Kapitel des Römerbriefs," Exegese im Methodenkonflikt. Zwischen Geschichte und Struktur, ed. by X. Leon-Dufour (Munich: Kösel, 1973) 73-116. J. A. Sanford interprets Rom 7:14-26 (unconvincingly) as showing that Paul had some degree of awareness of the Shadow, but repressed it himself and called for others to do so (Evil: The Shadow Side of Reality [New York: Crossroad, 1981] 69-76). W. A. Miller argues similarly in Make Friends With Your Shadow: How to Accept and Use Positively the Negative Side of Your Personality (Minneapolis: Augsburg, 1981) 72-80.

[6]The best treatment of the origin and development of this humoral psychology is that of R. Klibansky, E. Panofsky and F. Saxl, Saturn and Melancholy: Studies in the History of Natural Philosophy, Religion and Art (New York: Basic, 1964) 3-66. According to Klibansky et al., Galen (c. 130-200) was responsible for the first systematic statement of the psychological significance of the humors (pp. 57-8), but the ideas which he systematizes had been in the making at least since 500 BCE (pp. 4-57). One indication of this is the earlier use of the words referring to the individual humors. Thus for example, cholotos (bilious) = angry in Homer, Iliad 4.241 and Odyssey 22.26; phlegmatodes and cholodes are given a psychological meaning in Hippocrates, The Divine Disease; and melagcholikos is understood psychologically in Aristotle, Problems 30.1

[7]C. Brenner, An Elementary Textbook of Psychoanalysis. Revised Edition (Garden City, NY: Doubleday, 1974) 194.

[8]I. B. Myers and P. Myers, Gifts Differing (Palo Alto, CA: Consulting Psychologists Press, 1980) especially pp. 83-116.

[9]Ibid. 93.

BIBLIOGRAPHY   (Works Cited)

Africa, T. W., "The Mask of an Assassin: A Psychohistorical Study of M. Junius Brutus," Journal of
Interdisciplinary History 8 (1978) 599-626.

_____, "Psychohistory, Ancient History, and Freud:
The Descent into Avernus," Arethusa 12 (1979) 5-
33.

Anderson, J. W., "The Methodology of Psychological
Biography," Journal of Interdisciplinary History
11 (1981) 455-75.

Ariès, P., The Hour of Our Death trans. by H. Weaver
(New York: Knopf, 1981).

_____, Western Attitudes Toward Death: From the
Middle Ages to the Present trans. by P. M. Ranum
(The Johns Hopkins Symposia in Comparative
History; Baltimore: Johns Hopkins, 1974).

The Babylonian Talmud (London: Soncino, 1935-52).

Bailey, R. E., "Is 'Sleep' the Proper Biblical Term for
the Intermediate State?" ZNW 55 (1964) 161-7.

Balch, D. L., "1 Cor 7:32-5 and Stoic Debates about
Marriage, Anxiety and Distraction," JBL 102 (1983)
429-39.

Baldwin, A., "Personal Structure Analysis: A
Statistical Method for Investigating the Single
Personality," Journal of Abnormal and Social
Psychology 37 (1942) 163-83.

Barrett, C. K., The First Epistle to the Corinthians
(New York: Harper and Row, 1968).

_____, The Second Epistle to the Corinthians (New
York: Harper and Row, 1973).

Batey, R., "The MIA SARX Union of Christ and the
Church," NTS 13 (1967) 270-81.

_____, NT Nuptial Imagery (Leiden: Brill, 1971).

_____, "Paul's Bride Image. A Symbol of Realistic
Eschatology," Int 17 (1963) 176-82.

Beardslee, W. A., Human Achievement and Divine Vocation
    in the Message of Paul (SBT 31; Naperville, IL:
    Allenson, 1961).

Beker, J. C., Paul the Apostle: The Triumph of God in
    Life and Thought (Philadelphia: Fortress, 1980).

Bertram, G., "nepios ktl.," TDNT 4.912-23.

_____, "odin ktl.," TDNT 9.671.

Best, E., One Body in Christ: A Study of the
    Relationship of the Church to Christ in the
    Epistles of the Apostle Paul (London: SPCK,
    1955).

_____, Paul and His Converts: The Sprunt Lectures
    1985 (Edinburgh: T. & T. Clark, 1988).

Betz, H. D., Der Apostel Paulus und die sokratische
    Tradition: Eine exegetische Untersuchung zu
    seiner "Apologie" 2 Korinther 10-13 (BHT 45;
    Tübingen: Mohr [Siebeck], 1972).

_____, "Eine Christus-Aretalogie bei Paulus," ZThK
    66 (1969) 288-305.

_____, "De Laude Ipsius (Moralia 539 A - 547 F),"
    Plutarch's Ethical Writings and Early Christian
    Literature ed. by H. D. Betz (SCHNT 4; Leiden:
    Brill, 1978) 367-93.

_____, Galatians (Hermeneia; Philadelphia:
    Fortress, 1979).

Bishop, J. G., "Psychological Insights in St. Paul's
    Mysticism," Theology 78 (1975) 318-24.

Black, C. Clifton, "Pauline Perspectives on Death in
    Romans 5-8," JBL 103 (1984) 413-33.

Brenner, C., An Elementary Textbook of Psychoanalysis.
    Revised Edition (Garden City, NY: Doubleday,
    1974).

Brown, P., The Body and Society: Men, Women and Sexual
    Renunciation in Early Christianity (Lectures on
    the History of Religions, new series, 13; New
    York: Columbia University Press, 1988).

Bultmann, R., "Exegetische Probleme des 2. Korinther briefes," Exegetica. Aufsätze zur Erforschung des NT ed. by E. Dinkler (Tübingen: Mohr (Siebeck), 1967) 298-322 [original publication 1948].

_____, "kauchaomai ktl.," TDNT 3.648-52.

_____, "thanatos ktl.," TDNT 3.7-25.

_____, Theology of the NT (New York: Scribner, 1951, 1955).

_____, "zao ktl. D: The Concept of Life in Judaism," TDNT 2.855-61.

Callan, T., "The Saying of Jesus in Gos. Thom. 22/2 Clem. 12/Gos. Eg. 5," forthcoming in JRS.

Capps, D., "Augustine as Narcissist: Comments on Paul Rigby's 'Paul Ricoeur, Freudianism, and Augustine's Confessions,'" JAAR 53 (1985) 115-27.

Carrington, P., The Early Christian Church, 2 vols. (Cambridge: University Press, 1957).

Cassirer, H. W., Grace and Law: St. Paul, Kant and the Hebrew Prophets (Grand Rapids, MI: Eerdmans/Edinburgh: Handsel, 1988).

Cheek, J. L., "Paul's Mysticism in the Light of Psychedelic Experience," JAAR 38 (1970) 381-9.

Collange, J. -F., Enigmes de la Deuxieme Epitre de Paul aux Corinthians. Etude Exegetique de 2 Cor 2:14-7:4 (Cambridge: University Press, 1972).

Conzelmann, H., 1 Corinthians trans. by J. W. Leitch (Hermeneia; Philadelphia: Fortress, 1975).

Cox, D., Jung and St. Paul: A Study of the Doctrine of Justification by Faith and its Relation to the Concept of Individuation (London: Longmans, Green, 1959).

Créspy, G., "Exegèse et psychoanalyse. Considerations aventueuses sur Romains 7,7-25," L'evangile, hier et aujourd'hui. Mélanges offerts au Prof. Franz-J. Leenhardt (Geneva: Labor et Fides, 1968) 169-79.

Cumont, F., After Life in Roman Paganism (Silliman
　　Memorial Lectures; New Haven:　Yale, 1922).

Dahl, N. A., "The Atonement - An Adequate Reward for
　　the Akedah?" The Crucified Messiah and Other
　　Essays (Minneapolis:　Augsburg, 1974) 146-60.

_____, "Paul and the Church at Corinth According to
　　1 Corinthians 1:10-4:21," Studies in Paul
　　(Minneapolis:　Augsburg, 1977) 40-61.

Davies, D. M., "Free from the Law:　An Exposition of
　　the Seventh Chapter of Romans,"　Int 7 (1953) 156-
　　62.

De Boer, P. A. H., Fatherhood and Motherhood in
　　Israelite and Judean Piety (Leiden:　Brill, 1974).

de Boer, W. P., The Imitation of Paul:　An Exegetical
　　Study (Amsterdam:　Kampen, 1962).

Deissmann, A., Paul:　A Study in Social and Religious
　　History, trans. W. E. Wilson, 2nd ed. (London:
　　Hodder and Stoughton, 1926 [German original
　　1911]).

Dodd, C. H., "The Mind of Paul I," NT Studies
　　(Manchester:　University Press, 1953) 67-82
　　[original publication 1933].

_____, "The Mind of Paul II," NT Studies, 83-128.

Dodds, E. R., "Augustine's Confessions:　A Study in
　　Spiritual Maladjustment," Hibbert Journal 26
　　(1927) 459-73.

_____, The Greeks and the Irrational (Sather
　　Classical Lectures, 25; Berkeley:　University of
　　California Press, 1959).

Droge, A. J., "Mori lucrum:　Paul and Ancient Theories
　　of Suicide," NovT 30 (1988) 263-86.

Dupont, J., "The Conversion of Paul and its Influence
　　on his Understanding of Salvation by Faith,"
　　Apostolic History and the Gospel, ed. by W. W.
　　Gasque and R. P. Martin (Grand Rapids, MI:
　　Eerdmans, 1970) 176-94.

Elliott, J. H., A Home for the Homeless: A Sociological Exegesis of 1 Peter, Its Situation and
Strategy (Philadelphia: Fortress, 1981).

Erikson, E. H., Identity and the Life Cycle (New York:
Norton, 1979).

_____, "On the Nature of Psycho-Historical Evidence:
In Search of Gandhi," Daedalus 97 (1968) 695-730.

_____, Young Man Luther: A Study in Psychoanalysis
and History (New York: Norton, 1958).

Fiore, B., The Function of Personal Example in the
Socratic and Pastoral Epistles (AnBib 105; Rome:
Biblical Institute, 1986).

Fischer, H., Gespaltener christlicher Glaube: Eine
psychoanalytisch orientierte Religionskritik
(Hamburg: Reich, 1974).

Fitzgerald, J. T., Cracks in an Earthen Vessel: An
Examination of the Catalogues of Hardships in the
Corinthian Correspondence (SBLDS 99; Atlanta:
Scholars, 1988).

Forbes, C., "Comparison, Self-Praise and Irony: Paul's
Boasting and the Conventions of Hellenistic
Rhetoric," NTS 32 (1986) 1-30.

Forsyth, J. J., "Faith and Eros: Paul's Answer to
Freud," Religion in Life 46 (1977) 476-87.

Foucault, M., The History of Sexuality trans. by R.
Hurley; vol. 2: The Use of Pleasure (New York:
Pantheon, 1985); vol 3: The Care of the Self (New
York: Pantheon, 1986).

Fredriksen, P., "Augustine and his Analysts: The
Possibility of a Psychohistory," Soundings 61
(1978) 206-27.

_____, "Paul and Augustine: Conversion Narratives,
Orthodox Traditions, and the Retrospective Self,"
JTS 37 (1986) 3-34.

Freud, S., "Anxiety and Instinctual Life," New
Introductory Lectures on Psychoanalysis, reprinted
in The Standard Edition of the Complete

Psychological Works of Sigmund Freud ed. by J.
Strachey (London: Hogarth, 1964) 22.81-111.

_____, Beyond the Pleasure Principle, reprinted in
Standard Edition 18.1-64.

_____, "The Dissection of the Psychical
Personality," New Introductory Lectures on
Psychoanalysis, reprinted in Standard Edition
22.57-80.

_____, Moses and Monotheism reprinted in Standard
Edition 23.1-137.

_____, Three Essays on the Theory of Sexuality
reprinted in Standard Edition 7.123-245.

Fromm, E., The Anatomy of Human Destructiveness (New
York, Chicago, San Francisco: Holt, Rinehart &
Winston, 1973).

_____, "Die Entstehung des Christusdogmas. Eine
psychoanalytische Studie zur socialpsychologischen
Funktion der Religion," Imago 16 (1930) 305-73.

Furnish, V. P., II Corinthians (AB 32A; Garden City,
NY: Doubleday, 1984).

Gaventa, B., Paul's Conversion: A Critical Sifting of
the Epistolary Evidence (Duke University
dissertation, 1978).

_____, "'Where Then Is Boasting?': Romans 3:27 and
Its Contexts," Proceedings of the Eastern Great
Lakes Biblical Society 5 (1985) 57-66.

Gay, P., Freud for Historians (New York/Oxford: Oxford
University Press, 1985).

Gilmore, W. J., Psychohistorical Inquiry: A
Comprehensive Research Bibliography (Garland
Reference Library of Social Science, 156; New York
and London: Garland, 1984).

Gruber, M. I., "The Motherhood of God in Second
Isaiah," RB 90 (1983) 351-9.

Gruman, G. J., "Ethics of Death and Dying: Historical
Perspective," Omega 9 (1978-9) 203-37.

Grundmann, W., "Die NEPIOI in der urchristlichen
    Paränese," NTS 5 (1958-9) 188-205.

Gundry, R. H., "The Moral Frustration of Paul Before
    his Conversion: Sexual Lust in Romans 7:7-25,"
    Pauline Studies: Essays Presented to Professor F.
    F. Bruce on his 70th Birthday ed. by D. A. Hagner
    and M. J. Harris (Grand Rapids, MI: Eerdmans,
    1980) 28-45.

Gutierrez, P., La Paternité Spirituelle selon Saint
    Paul (Études Bibliques; Paris: Gabalda, 1968).

Hay, D. M., "Paul's Indifference to Authority," JBL 88
    (1969) 36-44.

Hengel, M., The Atonement: The Origins of the Doctrine
    in the NT trans. by J. Bowden (Philadelphia:
    Fortress, 1981).

_____, The Son of God: The Origin of Christology
    and the History of Jewish-Hellenistic Religion
    (Philadelphia: Fortress, 1976).

Hock, R. F., The Social Context of Paul's Ministry:
    Tentmaking and Apostleship (Philadelphia:
    Fortress, 1980).

Holtz, T., "Zum Selbstverständnis des Apostels Paulus,"
    TLZ 91 (1966) 321-30.

Holtzmann, H. J., Lehrbuch der neutestamentlichen
    Theologie, 2nd ed., 2 vols. (Freiburg: J. C. B.
    Mohr, 1897).

Hübner, H., "Boasting and Refraining from Boasting,"
    Law in Paul's Thought trans. by J. C. G. Greig
    (Edinburgh: T. & T. Clark, 1984) 101-24.

Inglis, C. G., "The Problem of St. Paul's Conversion,"
    ExpTim 40 (1928-29) 227-31.

Judge, E. A., "Paul's Boasting in Relation to
    Contemporary Professional Practice," AusBR 16
    (1968) 37-50.

Jung, C. G., "The Psychological Foundation of Belief in
    Spirits," Proceedings of the Society for Psychical
    Research 31 (1920), reprinted in The Collected
    Works of C. G. Jung, ed. by H. Read, M. Fordham,

G. Adler, 17 vols. (New York: Pantheon, 1960)
8.307-8.

Käsemann, E., Commentary on Romans trans. by G. W.
Bromiley (Grand Rapids, MI: Eerdmans, 1980).

_____, "Die Legitimät des Apostels. Eine
Untersuchung zu II Korinther 10-13," ZNW 41 (1942)
33-71.

_____, "A Pauline Version of the 'Amor Fati,'" NT
Questions of Today trans. by W. J. Montague
(Philadelphia: Fortress, 1969) 217-35.

Karris, R. J., Review of J. Sánchez Bosch, "Gloriarse"
segun San Pablo, JBL 92 (1973) 144-6.

Keck, L. E., "New Testament Views of Death,"
Perspectives on Death ed. by L. O. Mills
(Nashville and New York: Abingdon, 1969) 33-98.

Klibansky, R., E. Panofsky and F. Saxl, Saturn and
Melancholy: Studies in the History of Natural
Philosophy, Religion and Art (New York: Basic,
1964).

Knox, W. L., St. Paul and the Church of Jerusalem
(Cambridge: University Press, 1925).

Kohut, H., "Beyond the Bounds of the Basic Rule,"
Journal of the American Psychoanalytic Association
8 (1960) 567-86.

Lane Fox, R., Pagans and Christians (New York: Knopf,
1987).

Lambrecht, J., "Why Is Boasting Excluded? A Note on
Rom 3:27 and 4:2," ETL 61 (1985) 365-9.

LaPorte, J., "The Ages of Life in Philo of Alexandria,"
SBLSP 1986, 278-90.

Lull, D. J., "'The Law Was Our Pedagogue:' A Study in
Galatians 3:19-25," JBL 105 (1986) 489-95.

Lutz, C. E., Musonius Rufus "The Roman Socrates" (Yale
Classical Studies 10; New Haven: Yale, 1947).

MacDonald, D. R., "Ritual, Sex and Veils at Corinth,"
There Is No Male and Female: The Fate of a

Dominical Saying in Paul and Gnosticism (HDR 20;
Philadelphia: Fortress, 1987) 65-111.

Mack, J. E., "Psychoanalysis and Historical Biography,"
Journal of the American Psychoanalytic Association
19 (1971) 143-79.

MacMullen, R., Paganism in the Roman Empire (New Haven
and London: Yale, 1981).

Malherbe, A. J., "'Gentle as a Nurse:' The Cynic
Background to 1 Thess 2," NovT 12 (1970) 203-17.

Malina, B. J., "The Individual and the Community -
Personality in the Social World of Early
Christianity," BTB 9 (1979) 126-38.

_____, The NT World: Insights from Cultural
Anthropology (Atlanta: John Knox, 1981).

Manuel, F. E., "The Use and Abuse of Psychology in
History," Daedalus 100 (1971) 187-212.

Maranon, G., Tiberius the Resentful Caesar trans. by W.
B. Wells (New York: Duell, Sloan and Pearce,
1956).

Martin, H., Jr. and J. E. Phillips, "Consolatio ad
Uxorem (Moralia 608 A - 612 B)," Plutarch's
Ethical Writings and Early Christian Literature
ed. by H. D. Betz (SCHNT 4; Leiden: Brill, 1978)
394-441.

Martin-Achard, R., From Death to Life: A Study of the
Development of the Doctrine of the Resurrection in
the Old Testament trans. by J. P. Smith (Edinburgh
and London: Oliver and Boyd, 1960).

Mattoon, M. A., Jungian Psychology in Perspective (New
York: Free Press, 1981).

McGiffert, A. C., A History of Christianity in the
Apostolic Age (New York: Scribner, 1906).

Meeks, W. A., The First Urban Christians: The Social
World of the Apostle Paul (New Haven and London:
Yale, 1983).

_____, "The Image of the Androgyne: Some Uses of a Symbol in Earliest Christianity," HR 13 (1973-4) 165-208.

Menoud, P. H., "Revelation and Tradition: The Influence of Paul's Conversion on his Theology," Int 7 (1953) 131-41.

Michel, O., "Zur Lehre vom Todesschlaf," ZNW 35 (1936) 285-90.

Miller, J. W., "Jesus' 'Age Thirty Transition': A Psychohistorical Probe," SBLSP 1985, 45-56.

Miller, W. A., Make Friends With Your Shadow: How to Accept and Use Positively the Negative Side of Your Personality (Minneapolis: Augsburg, 1981).

Moore, G. F., Judaism in the First Centuries of the Christian Era, the Age of the Tannaim (New York: Schocken, 1971) [original publication 1927, 1930].

Moxnes, H., "Honor, Shame and the Outside World in Paul's Letter to the Romans," The Social World of Formative Christianity and Judaism: Essays in Tribute to Howard Clark Kee ed. by J. Neusner et al. (Philadelphia: Fortress, 1988) 207-18.

Murphy - O'Connor, J., "'Being at Home in the Body We Are in Exile from the Lord' (2 Cor 5:6b)," RB 93 (1986) 214-21.

Myers, I. B., P. Myers, Gifts Differing (Palo Alto, CA: Consulting Psychologists Press, 1980).

Nickelsburg, G. W. E., Jr., Resurrection, Immortality and Eternal Life in Intertestamental Judaism (HTS 26; Cambridge, MA: Harvard, 1972).

Nock, A. D., St. Paul (New York: Harper, 1938).

Olson, S. N., Confidence Expressions in Paul: Epistolary Conventions and the Purpose of 2 Corinthians (Yale University dissertation, 1976).

_____, "Epistolary Uses of Expressions of Self-Confidence," JBL 103 (1984) 585-97.

_____, "Pauline Expressions of Confidence in His Addressees," CBQ 47 (1985) 282-95.

Palmer, D. W., "'To Die is Gain' (Philippians i 21),"
NovT 17 (1975) 203-18.

Perkins, P., Resurrection: New Testament Witness and
Contemporary Reflection (Garden City, NY:
Doubleday, 1984).

Pfister, O., Christianity and Fear: A Study in History
and in the Psychology and Hygiene of Religion
trans. by W. H. Johnston (London: Allen and
Unwin, 1948).

_____, "Die Entwicklung des Apostels Paulus: Eine
religionsgeschichtliche und psychologische
Skizze," Imago 6 (1920) 243-90.

Pfitzner, V. C., Paul and the Agon Motif: Traditional
Athletic Imagery in the Pauline Literature (NovT
Sup 16; Leiden: Brill, 1967).

Ridderbos, H., Paul: An Outline of His Theology,
trans. by J. R. DeWitt (Grand Rapids, MI:
Eerdmans, 1975).

Riddle, D. W., Paul. Man of Conflict: A Modern
Biographical Sketch (Nashville: Cokesbury, 1940).

Rigby, P., "Paul Ricoeur, Freudianism, and Augustine's
Confessions," JAAR 53 (1985) 93-114.

Robinson, J. A. T., The Body: A Study in Pauline
Theology (SBT 5; London: SCM, 1952).

Robinson, P. A., The Conception of Death in Judaism in
the Hellenistic and Early Roman Period (University
of Wisconsin - Madison dissertation, 1978).

Rohde, E., Psyche: The Cult of Souls and Belief in
Immortality Among the Greeks trans. by W. B. Hills
(New York: Harcourt, Brace, 1925) [original
publication 1897].

Rousselle, A., Porneia: On Desire and the Body in
Antiquity trans. by F. Pheasant (Family, Sexuality
and Social Relations in Past Times; New York:
Blackwell, 1988)

Rozelaar, M., "Seneca: A New Approach to his
Personality," Psychiatry 36 (1973) 82-92.

Rubenstein, R., My Brother Paul (New York: Harper and Row, 1972).

Sampley, J. P., 'And the Two Shall Become One Flesh': A Study of Traditions in Ephesians 5:21-33 (SNTSMS 16; Cambridge: University Press, 1971).

Sánchez Bosch, J., "Gloriarse" segun San Pablo: Sentido y teologia de kauchaomai (AnBib 40 and Colectanea San Paciano, 16; Rome: Biblical Institute/Barcelona: Facultad de Teologia (SSP), 1970).

Sanders, E. P., Paul and Palestinian Judaism: A Comparison of Patterns of Religion (Philadelphia: Fortress, 1977).

_____, Paul, the Law and the Jewish People (Philadelphia: Fortress, 1983).

Sandmel, S., The Genius of Paul: A Study in History (New York: Schocken, 1970).

Sanford, J. A., Evil: The Shadow Side of Reality (New York: Crossroad, 1981).

Schoeps, H. J., Paul: The Theology of the Apostle in the Light of Jewish Religious History trans. by H. Knight (Philadelphia: Westminster, 1961).

Schreiber, A., Die Gemeinde in Korinth. Versuch einer gruppendynamische Betrachtung der Entwicklung der Gemeinde von Korinth auf der Basis des ersten Korintherbriefes (Munster: Aschendorf, 1977).

Schrenk, G., G. Quell, "pater ktl.," TDNT 5.945-1022.

Schütz, J. H., Paul and the Anatomy of Apostolic Authority (SNTSMS 26; Cambridge: University Press, 1975).

Schweitzer, A., The Mysticism of Paul the Apostle trans. by W. Montgomery (New York: Holt, 1931).

Schweizer, E., "Dying and Rising with Christ," NTS 14 (1967) 1-14.

Scroggs, R., "The Heuristic Value of the Psychoanalytic Model in the Interpretation of Paul," Zygon 13 (1978) 136-57.

_____, The NT and Homosexuality: Contextual Background for Contemporary Debate (Philadelphia: Fortress, 1983).

_____, "Psychology as a Tool to Interpret the Text," The Christian Century, March 24, 1982, 335-8.

Selwyn, E. G., "St. Stephen's Place in Christian Origins," Theology 5 (1922) 306-16.

Silberman, L. H., "Death in the Hebrew Bible and Apocalyptic Literature," Perspectives on Death ed. by L. O. Mills (Nashville/New York: Abingdon, 1969) 13-32.

Spiegel, S., The Last Trial, trans. by J. Goldin (New York: Schocken, 1967).

Stendahl, K., "The Apostle Paul and the Introspective Conscience of the West," Paul Among Jews and Gentiles 78-96.

_____, Paul Among Jews and Gentiles (Philadelphia: Fortress, 1976).

Stollberg, D., "Tiefenpsychologie oder historisch-kritische Exegese? Identität und der Tod des Ich (Gal 2:19-20)," Doppeldeutlich. Tiefendimensionen biblischer Texte, ed. by Y. Spiegel (Munich: Kaiser, 1978) 215-26.

Stumpff, A., "zelos ktl.," TDNT 2.877-88.

Swidler, L., Biblical Affirmations of Women (Philadelphia: Westminster, 1979).

Tannehill, R., Dying and Rising with Christ: A Study in Pauline Theology (BZNW 32; Berlin: Töpelmann, 1967).

Tarachow, S., "St. Paul and Early Christianity: A Psychoanalytic and Historical Study," Psychoanalysis and the Social Sciences 4 (1955) 223-81.

Theissen, G., "Legitimation and Subsistence: An Essay on the Sociology of Early Christian Missionaries," The Social Setting of Pauline Christianity trans. by J. H. Schütz (Philadelphia: Fortress, 1982).

_____, Psychological Aspects of Pauline Theology, trans. by J. P. Galvin (Philadelphia: Fortress, 1987).

Thompson, J. G. S. S., "Sleep: An Aspect of Jewish Anthropology," VT 5 (1955) 421-33.

Thompson, R. W., "Paul's Double Critique of Jewish Boasting: A Study of Rom 3,27 in Its Context," Bib 67 (1986) 520-31.

Toynbee, A., "Traditional Attitudes Toward Death," in A. Toynbee et al., Man's Concern with Death (St. Louis, New York, San Francisco: McGraw-Hill, 1969) 59-94.

Trible, P., God and the Rhetoric of Sexuality (Overtures to Biblical Theology; Philadelphia: Fortress, 1978).

Troeger K. -W., et. al., "Die sechste und siebte Schrift aus Nag Hammadi-Codex VI," TLZ 98 (1973) 495-503.

Vanhoye, A., "Personnalité de Paul et exégèse paulinienne," L'Apotre Paul: Personnalité, Style et Conception du Ministère ed. by A. Vanhoye (Leuven: University Press, 1986).

Vergote, A., "Der Beitrag der Psychoanalyse zur Exegese. Leben, Gesetz und Ich-Spaltung im 7. Kapitel des Römerbriefs," Exegese im Methodenkonflikt. Zwischen Geschichte und Struktur, ed. by X. Leon-Dufour (Munich: Kösel, 1973) 73-116.

Vermes, G., "Redemption and Genesis XXII," Scripture and Tradition (Leiden: Brill, 1961) 193-227.

von Rad, G., "zao ktl. B. 2: Death in the OT," TDNT 2.846-9.

Wedderburn, A. J. M., "The Soteriology of the Mysteries and Pauline Baptismal Theology," NovT 29 (1987) 53-72.

Wellisch, E., "The Oedipus Conflict in the Akedah," Isaac and Oedipus (London: Routledge and Kegan Paul, 1954) 74-97.

Wengst, K., Humility: Solidarity of the Humiliated.
    The Transformation of an Attitude and its Social
    Relevance in Graeco-Roman, Old Testament-Jewish
    and Early Christian Tradition trans. by J. Bowden
    (Philadelphia: Fortress, 1988).

Wikenhauser, A., Die Kirche als der mystische Leib
    Christi nach dem Apostel Paulus (Münster:
    Aschendorff, 1937).

Williams, S. K., Jesus' Death as Saving Event: The
    Background and Origin of a Concept (HDR 2;
    Missoula, MT: Scholars, 1975).

Wimbush, V. L., Paul the Worldly Ascetic: Response to
    the World and Self-Understanding according to 1
    Corinthians (Macon, GA: Mercer, 1987).

Yarbrough, O. L., Not Like the Gentiles: Marriage
    Rules in the Letters of Paul (SBLDS 80; Atlanta:
    Scholars, 1985).

Yerkes, R. K., Sacrifice in Greek and Roman Religions
    and Early Judaism (Hale Lectures; New York:
    Scribner, 1952).

Zeligs, D. F., Psychoanalysis and the Bible: A Study
    in Depth of Seven Leaders (New York: Human
    Sciences Press, 1988).

INDEX OF REFERENCES

A. Biblical References

B. Jewish Literature

C. Christian Literature

F. Modern Authors

STUDIES IN THE BIBLE AND EARLY CHRISTIANITY